How to Prepare For the STATE STANDARDS

VOL. 2

2nd Grade Edition

By Nancy Samuels

CARNEY EDUCATIONAL SERVICES

Helping Students Help Themselves

Special thanks to Rim Namkoong, our illustrator

This book is dedicated to:

The moms and dads who get up early and stay up late. You are the true heroes, saving our future, one precious child at a time.

All the kids who don't make the evening news. To the wide-eyed children, full of love, energy, and wonder. You are as close to perfection as this world will ever see.

TABLE OF CONTENTS

Introduction for Parents

The Focus and Purpose of this Book

Many states have recently adopted rigorous academic content standards for students in grades K – 12. The content standards set forth exactly what students need to learn in each grade level in language arts, mathematics, history-social science, and science. This book presents exercises that test student mastery of each of the academic content standards.

In conjunction with the standards, many states have initiated standardized testing programs. As a part of these programs, students take nationally normed achievement tests designed by the state to assess how well the students have mastered the skills and information covered in the state standards. The results give teachers, parents, and students invaluable information about a child's relative academic strengths and the next steps for learning.

The purpose of this book is twofold: (1) to assist students in mastering the information addressed in each of the content standards, and (2) to prepare students to perform their best on the appropriate standardized test. It is designed for student use in the classroom or for support of classroom lessons. The book is divided into "practice skill" sections that correlate to the various strands of the content standards. Each section is introduced with a statement of expectations for student learning in the practice skill area. Every section also contains tips and strategies to help the student learn the information or reason through the exercises. The exercises are presented in various formats that will give the students practice in answering questions much like those that they are likely to encounter on any standardized nationally normed test.

Academic Content Standards in Grade 2

By the end of grade 2, students are expected to achieve mastery in several areas. The major areas of focus are listed below.

LANGUAGE ARTS areas of focus include:
- Reading Vocabulary
  - Read aloud fluently, including multisyllable words
  - Recognize plurals and common abbreviations
  - Understand antonyms, synonyms, and words with multiple meanings
  - Know meaning of compound words and affixes and use them to determine the meaning of new words

- Reading Comprehension
  - Use titles, tables of contents, and chapter headings to locate information
  - Restate facts and details in informational text
  - Organize information
  - Recognize cause-and-effect relationships
  - Interpret information from charts and diagrams
  - Follow two-step written instructions

- Literary Response and Analysis
  - Understand various plots, settings, and characters
  - Analyze alternative endings
  - Identify the use of rhythm, rhyme, and alliteration in poetry
- Listening and Speaking
  - Listen critically and ask questions for clarification and explanation
  - Give and follow 3- and 4-step directions
  - Paraphrase oral information
  - Retell stories and describe story elements, including characters, setting, and plot
  - Report on a topic with supportive facts and details
- Writing Strategies and Applications
  - Write clear and coherent sentences
  - Write paragraphs that develop a central idea
  - Group related ideas and maintain a consistent focus
  - Recognize the different purposes of writing (describe, explain, persuade, tell a story)
  - Work through the writing process of prewriting, drafting, revising, and editing; revise to improve sequence and add descriptive detail
  - Use a dictionary, thesaurus, and atlas
  - Write brief narratives based on an experience; present events in logical sequence and describe setting, characters, objects, and events in detail
  - Write a friendly letter with date, salutation, body, closing, and signature
- Written and Oral English Language Conventions
  - Distinguish between complete and incomplete sentences
  - Recognize and use the correct word order in written sentences
  - Identify and correctly use parts of speech (nouns and verbs)
  - Use commas and quotation marks correctly
  - Capitalize all proper nouns, words at the beginning of sentences and greetings, months and days of the week, and titles and initials of people
  - Spell frequently used, irregularly spelled words correctly
  - Spell basic short-vowel, long-vowel, *r*-controlled, and consonant-blend patterns correctly

MATHEMATICS areas of focus include:
- Number Sense
  - Count, read, and write whole numbers to 1,000 and understand place value for each digit
  - Represent numbers in expanded notation to 1,000
  - Order and compare whole numbers to 1,000, using the symbols >, <, =
  - Add and subtract two- and three-digit numbers
  - Understand the concepts of multiplication and division
  - Know the multiplication tables of 2s, 5s, and 10s by memory
  - Understand the concepts of fractions and decimals
  - Recognize, name, and compare unit fractions
  - Solve addition and subtraction problems involving money; know the value of various coins and bills

- o Use estimation strategies in computation and problem solving
- Algebra and Functions
  - o Use number sentences involving addition and subtraction to solve problems
  - o Use data from charts, graphs and number sentences to solve problems
  - o Use the commutative and associative rules to check results
- Measurement and Geometry
  - o Measure length of objects by repeating standard and nonstandard units
  - o Measure to the nearest inch and/or centimeter
  - o Tell time to the nearest quarter hour; know relationships of time (minutes in an hour, days in a month, weeks in a year)
  - o Determine duration of intervals of time in hours
  - o Identify, describe and classify plane and solid geometric figure shapes
- Statistics, Data Analysis, and Probability
  - o Collect numerical data and record, organize, display, and interpret the data on various charts and graphs
  - o Identify the range and mode of data sets
  - o Recognize, describe, and extend linear patterns
- Mathematical Reasoning
  - o Make decisions about how to set up a problem; use appropriate problem solving strategies

HISTORY-SOCIAL SCIENCE areas of focus include:
- People Who Have Made a Difference
  - o Differentiate between things that happened long ago and things that happened recently
  - o Understand a time line
  - o Compare and contrast our daily lives with those of our parents and grandparents
- Map Skills
  - o Label from memory on a map of North America the countries, oceans, Great Lakes, major rivers, and mountain ranges
  - o Identify essential map elements
- Governmental Institutions in the U.S. and Other Countries
  - o Explain how the U.S. and other countries make laws, carry them out, determine whether laws have been violated, and punish wrongdoers
  - o Describe the ways countries interact with each other and try to solve problems (trade, cultural contacts, treaties, diplomacy, and military force)
- Economic Concepts
  - o Understand basic economic concepts (production, consumption; interdependence of buyers and sellers of goods and services)
  - o Understand how limits of resources affect our lives
- Concepts of Character
  - o Understand the importance of individual action
  - o Understand the importance of character
  - o Study the biographies of and explain how heroes from long ago and the recent past have made a difference in others' lives

SCIENCE areas of focus include:

- Physical Sciences
  - Know basic concepts of the motion of objects (push and pull forces, gravity)
  - Know that magnets can be used to make some objects move without being touched
  - Know sound is made by vibrating objects and can be described by its pitch and volume
- Life Sciences
  - Know the predictable life cycle of plants and animals, including butterflies, frogs, and mice
  - Understand the effects of light, gravity, touch , or environmental stress on plants
  - Know the role of flowers and fruits in plant reproduction
- Earth Sciences
  - Know the compositions of rocks and compare the physical properties of different rocks
  - Know the composition, properties, and importance of soil
  - Understand fossil formation and know how scientists use fossils
  - Know the resources of our earth and human use of those resources
- Investigation and Experimentation
  - Develop questions and perform investigations; record data
  - Make predictions based on observations
  - Measure length, weight, temperature, and liquid volume with appropriate tools
  - Express measurement in standard metric system units

Subjects Tested on Standardized Tests in Grade 2

Students in grade 2 are tested in language arts and mathematics. The language arts portion of the test includes questions that measure word study skills (reading and analyzing words using elements of phonics, syllables, and other word parts), reading vocabulary (synonyms, determining word meanings in context), reading comprehension (textual, recreational, and functional materials), spelling, language (elements of grammar, alphabetical order), listening skills, and study skills. The math sections of the test measure student mastery of the same concepts that are the focus of the academic content standards: number sense, math facts and procedures, whole number computation, fraction and decimal concepts, geometry and measurement, patterns and relationships, statistics and probability, and problem solving strategies. To date, many states have not required elementary schools to administer a standardized test to measure student achievement in history-social science or science. It is anticipated that there will be such a requirement in the near future.

Test Taking Strategies for Students in Grade 2

Students in grade 2 receive their own test booklets in which to read the questions and fill in a bubble next to their answer choice. The bubbling marks are the only ones that they will be allowed to make on the tests. For the math sections, however, students may use scratch paper. No calculators are allowed. In fact, to ensure the integrity of the testing, during the testing period teachers must remove all charts and diagrams relevant to the subject of the test.

► Listen Carefully, Bubble Accurately, and Keep Up With the Pace

An important aspect of the test is that a student must listen carefully and pay close attention to the teacher before, during, and after the test. The teacher will give oral instructions about the test and will read parts of the test to the students. The teacher's words are scripted, and the script sets strict limits on the number of times instructions and test questions may be repeated. A student must remain attentive, keep track of the number of the question that they are answering, and make sure to keep up with the pace.

► Eliminate Any Unreasonable Answer Choices and Select the Best Answer

In a test with a multiple-choice format, it is sometimes difficult to find the "perfect" answer among the choices given. First, eliminate all obviously wrong choices in order to concentrate on the remaining ones. Ultimately, it may be difficult to choose between two choices. In such instances, the student should reread the question carefully. It will likely contain key words needed to select the best answer. It may be the case that two choices are factually correct, but one choice more directly answers the question than another. Consider the following example:

Read the passage and answer the question about it.

Dogs are members of the canine family. They come in a variety of breeds and hundreds of different shapes and sizes. Each breed has its own special talent. Sheep dogs herd cattle and sheep. Golden retrievers make good guide dogs for the blind. St. Bernards are famous for rescuing people in the mountains. Huskies pull sleds to transport people and supplies over frozen terrain.

1. What is the main idea of this selection?

> o   a. All dogs are canines.
> o   b. All dogs look the same.
> o   c. Dogs make good companions.
> o   d. Different dog breeds have special talents.

To select the best answer, first eliminate the obviously incorrect choice "b." Although the remaining choices are all true statements, and even though choice "a" is taken directly from the selection, only choice "d" addresses the main idea of the passage. Choice "d" is the best answer.

▶Solve Math Problems on Scratch Paper. Work Neatly and Keep Organized.

Students may not make marks in the test booklet, except to bubble in their answers. Teachers will distribute scratch paper for solving problems. It will be important to transfer the problem accurately onto the scratch paper, align columns, and keep track of what problem is being solved. This means that the student will need to pay extra attention to neatness, organization, and accuracy. Time is often a factor in math tests, so it is will be necessary to work steadily and focus on the task at hand. If the student is really stumped on one problem, it may be best to give an educated guess, make a notation about the problem number, and return to it later if time permits. Any questions left unanswered will be counted wrong, so it is best not to spend too much time on any one problem. There is probably a question waiting down the line that will be much easier to solve!

Introduction for Students

About This Book

Your state has developed a set of guidelines (called "academic content standards") for students in every grade, from Kindergarten through grade 12. These standards tell us exactly what students need to learn in each grade level in language arts, math, history-social studies, and science. The exercises in this book follow the standards for second grade. As you complete these exercises, you will be able to tell which standards you have learned and which areas you might want to review.

In order to know how well children are learning the information they need to know, all students take certain tests every year usually in the spring. In second grade, students take tests in language arts and math. The exercises in this book will help you get ready for these tests. They will give you practice in answering questions about the things that you will need to know by the end of second grade.

This book is divided into four sections, one for each of the subjects where there are established standards: language arts, math, history-social studies, and science. Each section is divided into practice skill areas that explain what students are expected to know within the particular standard. Look for the box of tips in each section. The tips will explain special ways to remember the information, or will give you help in working through the exercises.

What You Will Learn in the Second Grade

In the second grade you will accomplish many things. Here are some of them.

Language Arts - You will read silently and read aloud with understanding. You will learn the meaning of many new words. You will analyze poetry, stories, and books that give you new information. You will organize your thoughts to speak and write about various topics in a way that is clear to others.

Math – You will work with numbers from 1 to 1,000. Although the focus will be on addition and subtraction, you will learn about multiplication and division, too.

History-Social Studies – The theme for the year is "People Who Have Made a Difference." You will compare and contrast your life with the lives of others who live in different places or lived in different times. You will learn more about North America, the United States, and your state.

Science – One area of focus is the study of objects in motion. You will also learn about the life cycles of plants and animals. Second grade students also study rocks, minerals, and fossils. In learning about these topics, you will question, observe, predict, investigate, experiment, and record data. You will be a scientist!

Test Taking Tips

1. **Read for 20 minutes every day.** The skills that you use to read are the same skills that will help you to do well on any test.

2. **Review a little every day.** If you practice or review what you have already learned in class, it will help you to remember the information when it appears on a test. It is easier and more effective to learn something in six 10-minute sessions that in one hour-long session.

3. **When solving math problems, work neatly and keep organized.** Take extra care when you are writing problems or transferring answers from scratch paper to an answer column or test booklet. You must copy the problems accurately and compute accurately. It helps to work each problem in its own area, separated from another problem. Be sure to align columns correctly. This will help you to avoid careless errors.

4. **Stay focused.** Often, you will only have a limited time to complete a test. Other times you will need to listen to oral instructions or respond to what you hear. Be sure to concentrate on the task at hand. Keep working and don't let your mind wander. If you don't know an answer, be sure not to spend so much time on that one question that you can't finish the rest of the test. Consider taking an educated guess or skipping the question and coming back to work on it after you have completed the rest of the test.

5. **In multiple-choice tests, eliminate obviously wrong choices and select the best answer.** Sometimes it is difficult to find the "perfect" answer among the choices given. The first thing to do is eliminate the choices that are obviously wrong and concentrate on the remaining ones. If you find it difficult to choose between two choices that both seem correct, go back and reread the question very carefully. Look for key words that will help you focus on the best choice. Don't be fooled by choices that are true, but that do not directly answer the question! Here is an example:

Read the passage and answer the question about it.

Dogs are members of the canine family. They come in a variety of breeds and hundreds of different shapes and sizes. Each breed has its own special talent. Sheep dogs herd cattle and sheep. Golden retrievers make good guide dogs for the blind. St. Bernards are famous for rescuing people in the mountains. Huskies pull sleds to transport people and supplies over frozen terrain.

1. What is the main idea of this selection?

   o a. All dogs are canines.
   o b. All dogs look the same.
   o c. Dogs make good companions.
   ⊚ d. Different dog breeds have special talents.

To select the best answer, first eliminate the obviously incorrect choice "b." Although the remaining choices are all true statements, and even though choice "a" is stated in the paragraph, only choice "d" tells the main idea of the paragraph. Choice "d" is the correct answer.

6.   Take some practice tests so you won't be nervous. The more you get used to thinking about what you know and answering questions about it, the more comfortable and confident you can be. A positive attitude is always the best way to approach learning and testing. The exercises in this book are designed to help you learn what you need to know in second grade and to practice answering questions about it. You will be able to say, "I know how to do this. I do it all the time!"

NOTES

LANGUAGE ARTS

Practice Skill: READING COMPREHENSION

Expectation: Be a careful and accurate reader. Think about what you are reading. Keep asking yourself, "Does this make sense?"

Tip: Good readers think about what they are reading. When they read something new, they look at pictures, titles, and key words to get an idea about what they will read. When they come to a word they don't know, they think of words that will make sense, and they try again. They use the rest of the words to help figure out the one they don't know.

PRACTICE ACTIVITY # 1

The Table of Contents below is from a book called <u>All About Famous Americans</u>. Use it to answer the questions.

ALL ABOUT FAMOUS AMERICANS

Table of Contents

Chapter 1	Presidents	Page 1
Chapter 2	Sports Heroes	Page 8
Chapter 3	Important Women	Page 12
Chapter 4	Scientists	Page 16
Chapter 5	Explorers	Page 20
Chapter 6	Artists and Musicians	Page 25

1. What page does chapter 4 begin on?
   - a. 12
   - ● b. 16
   - c. 20
   - d. 22

2. Where would you find information about Abraham Lincoln?
  ● a. Chapter 1
  ○ b. Chapter 2
  ○ c. Chapter 3
  ○ d. Chapter 4

3. What chapter would tell about Pocahontas and Susan B. Anthony?
  ○ a. Chapter 1
  ● b. Chapter 3
  ○ c. Chapter 4
  ○ d. Chapter 6

PRACTICE ACTIVITY # 2

Use the Table of Contents to answer the questions.

RABBITS MAKE GOOD PETS
Table of Contents

Chapter 1	Make a Hutch	Page 1
Chapter 2	Feeding Your Rabbit	Page 8
Chapter 3	Rabbit Habits	Page 14
Chapter 4	Grooming	Page 20
Chapter 5	Indoor or Outdoor?	Page 24
Chapter 6	Blue Ribbon Rabbits	Page 28

4. Which chapter might tell you what a rabbit likes to eat?
  ○ a. 1
  ○ b. 4
  ○ c. 5
  ● d. 2

5. Chapter six might tell you about
  ○ a. what a rabbit eats.
  ○ b. how to make a hutch.
  ● c. what a rabbit show is like and how to win a show.
  ○ d. grooming your rabbit.

6. What page might tell about how to keep your pet in your bedroom?
  ○ a. page 1
  ○ b. page 14
  ● c. page 24
  ○ d. page 28

ACTIVITY # 1

Read the following selection. Think about what you read. Then read the question and choose the best answer.

Jose loves the circus. Uncle Ramon takes him to see the show every time it comes to town. The clowns are so funny that Jose laughs until he cries. Uncle Ramon enjoys the trapeze artists who fly through the air. But their favorite act is the lion tamer who plays with the huge tigers and lions like they were his house pets. Jose and Uncle Ramon think he is quite brave.

1. What is this story mostly about?
   - o a. the circus clown
   - o b. Jose
   - ● c. circus acts that are fun to watch
   - o d. how the lion tamer works

2. What is Jose's favorite part of the show?
   - o a. the elephants
   - o b. the clowns
   - o c. the trapeze artists
   - ● d. the lion tamer

3. Which statement is true?
   - o a. The clowns are boring.
   - ● b. Uncle Ramon likes the trapeze act.
   - o c. This was Jose's first trip to the circus.
   - o d. Jose has a pet tiger.

4. What do Jose and Uncle Ramon think about the lion tamer?
   - o a. He is funny.
   - o b. He is crazy.
   - o c. He likes panthers.
   - ● d. None of the above

5. What does Uncle Ramon think about the clowns?
   - o a. He thinks they are funny.
   - o b. They are not as funny as the dancing bear.
   - o c. They are better than the lion tamer.
   - ● d. The story does not say.

ACTIVITY #2

Read the following selection. Think about what you read. Then read the question and choose the best answer.

Nothing tastes better than lemonade on a hot day. It's easy to make. Give it a try. Wash two lemons. Cut them in half and squeeze the lemon juice into a glass. Add a teaspoon of sugar. Pour water into the glass to fill it up. Stir it with a spoon and then take a sip. If it is too sour, sweeten it up a little more, or just drink it up and let your lips pucker.

1. What is a good title for this selection?
   o a. A Good Summer Business
   ● b. How to Make Lemonade
   o c. Lemons Are Sour
   o d. Making Lemonade is Hard to Do

2. What do you need to make lemonade?
   ● a. lemons, water, sugar
   o b. lemons, glass, salt
   o c. spoon, glass, bowl
   o d. none of the above

3. Why would you take a sip of the lemonade?
   o a. to save all the lemons
   o b. because you are very thirsty
   ● c. to see if it is sweet
   o d. because you are scared

4. When does the author like to drink lemonade?
   ● a. on a hot day
   o b. on a cold day
   o c. every night
   o d. with a dish of ice cream

5. When will your lips pucker?
   o a. when it is too sweet
   ● b. when it is too sour
   o c. when it is just right
   o d. none of the above

ACTIVITY #3

Read the following selection. Think about what you read. Then read the question and choose the best answer.

Sara and her brother had waited weeks for this day to come. They took their baseball gloves, grabbed the tickets, and jumped in the car. Their father drove them to the stadium. They ate hot dogs and ice cream as they watched the game. After the home team won, there were fireworks in the evening sky. It was a day they would remember for many years.

1. Where did Sara and her brother go?
   - ● a. to a baseball game
   - o b. to a football game
   - o c. to a birthday party
   - o d. on vacation

2. What word best describes how Sara and her brother felt?
   - o a. tired
   - o b. silly
   - ● c. excited
   - o d. confused

3. What did they do at the game?
   - o a. caught a fly ball
   - o b. talked to the pitcher
   - o c. forgot the tickets
   - o d. none of the above

4. Who took Sara to the game?
   - o a. her brother
   - o b. her mother
   - o c. her father
   - ● d. none of the above

5. What part of the story tells you the game ended in the night?
   - o a. They ate hot dogs and ice cream.
   - o b. They drove in the car.
   - ● c. There were fireworks in the evening sky.
   - o d. None of the above

ACTIVITY #4

Read the following short story. Think about what you read. Then read the questions and choose the best answer.

Once Tim went on a fishing trip with his grandma and grandpa. They awoke at dawn because Grandpa said, "We want to catch our breakfast. The early bird catches the worm." Tim was a little worried. If he didn't catch any fish, would he have to eat worms for breakfast? His mom smiled and told him not to worry. She packed Tim a sandwich to take along. It tasted good, but not as good as the trout they caught.

1. What is this story about?
   - o a. fishing poles
   - ◉ b. a fishing trip
   - o c. worms
   - o d. birds

2. When did Tim wake up to go fishing?
   - o a. at lunch time
   - o b. in the middle of the night
   - ◉ c. when the sun came up
   - o d. none of the above

3. What word best describes Tim's feelings?
   - o a. scared
   - o b. angry
   - ◉ c. worried
   - o d. happy

4. What did Tim take on the trip?
   - o a. trout
   - ◉ b. a sandwich
   - o c. a backpack
   - o d. his mother

5. What kind of fish did Tim catch?
   - o a. worm fish
   - o b. catfish
   - o c. bass
   - ◉ d. trout

ACTIVITY #5

Read the following selection. Think about what you read. Then read the question and choose the best answer.

Mavis always looks forward to a trip to her grandma's house in the country. Life on the farm is hard work, but Grandma always makes sure that she and Mavis have fun together. First, they pick apples off the trees. Then they cook them to make applesauce. They usually have enough left over to make a delicious dessert. This year Grandma taught Mavis how to bake the apples with sugar and cinnamon on top. It is a yummy treat. Next year Grandma and Mavis plan to make apple juice and apple butter. Mavis will bring some home to her friends in the city.

1. Where does Grandma live?
    o a. on a ranch in the country
    o b. near an airport
    o c. in the city
    ● d. on a farm in the country

2. Who lives in the city?
    o Grandma
    o Mavis
    ● Mavis and her friends
    o None of the above

3. What do Mavis and Grandma do first?
    o a. cook applesauce
    o b. bake apples
    o c. make apple juice
    ● d. pick apples from the trees

4. What did Grandma teach Mavis this year?
    ● a. to make baked apples
    o b. to make apple juice
    o c. to make apple pie
    o d. none of the above

5. Which statement is true?
    o a. Grandma loves apple juice.
    ● b. Mavis has friends who live in the city.
    o c. Mavis does not enjoy her farm visits.
    o d. Mavis and Grandma buy apples at the store.

Practice Skill: COMPREHENSION OF EXPOSITORY TEXT

Expectation: Read to learn new facts.

Tip: When you read nonfiction, you probably are reading to find out something or to learn some new fact. Before you start to read, think about what you already know about the subject and what you want to learn about it. Think of some questions that you will try to answer from your reading.

ACTIVITY # 1

Read the following selection. Think about what you read. Then read the question and choose the best answer.

If you ask most people, "What is a bird?" they will answer that it is an animal that can fly. But think carefully about this answer. A bee is an animal that can fly. But a bee is an insect, not a bird. A bat can fly, too. But bats are not birds. They are mammals. On the other hand, an ostrich, the world's largest bird, cannot fly at all. Even though the ostrich is so large—it can grow to be nine feet tall and weigh 350 pounds—it can run more than forty miles per hour. That is faster than any animal with two legs.

So what is a bird? A bird is a warm-blooded animal with a backbone, and it has wings, feathers, a beak, and no teeth.

Another important thing to know about birds is that they all lay eggs with hard shells. The ostrich lays the largest eggs. Their eggs can be seven inches long and weigh three pounds each. The smallest eggs belong to the smallest bird, the bee hummingbird. The bee hummingbird is only 2 ½ inches long from the tip of its beak to the end of its tail. Its egg is the size of your littlest fingernail.

1. Which of these animals is a bird?
   o a. bat
   o b. bee
   ⊙ c. ostrich
   o d. none of the above

2. Which statement is true?
   - ○ a. All birds fly.
   - ● b. All birds have feathers.
   - ○ c. All birds are slow runners.
   - ○ d. None of the above

3. What is the smallest bird?
   - ○ a. bee
   - ● b. bee hummingbird
   - ○ c. ostrich
   - ○ d. robin

4. Which of these animals is an insect?
   - ○ a. bat
   - ○ b. mammal
   - ● c. bee
   - ○ d. bird

5. How fast can an ostrich run?
   - ● a. 40 miles per hour
   - ○ b. 9 miles per hour
   - ○ c. 350 miles per hour
   - ○ d. none of the above

6. How big is a bee hummingbird?
   - ○ a. 7 inches long
   - ○ b. as long as your little fingernail
   - ● c. 2 ½ inches long
   - ○ d. none of the above

7. If you want to know if birds have teeth,
   - ○ a. you must read another article.
   - ● b. you can find it in this selection.
   - ○ c. you can ask your pet canary.
   - ○ d. none of the above

8. If you want to know if birds have knees,
   - ● a. you must read another article.
   - ○ b. you can find it in this selection.
   - ○ c. you can ask your pet canary.
   - ○ d. none of the above

ACTIVITY # 2

Do you dream of exploring the world and seeing places that few people have seen? Would you like to be a scientist in the land of penguins, seals, and whales? Would you like to have 24 hours of sunlight every summer day? Are you interested in visiting the South Pole? If your answer to these questions is "Yes!" then perhaps you should plan a visit to Antarctica.

In Antarctica, it is easier to visit in the summer than in the winter. In the summer, the temperature can be 30° F, but in the winter it is the coldest place in the world. Antarctic winds are fierce and strong. They can blow up to 100 miles per hour. They cause special blizzards called "white out" blizzards. In a white out blizzard the sky is clear and blue, no snow is falling, but snow is swirling so hard from the ground that all you can see is white all around you. It is easy to get lost.

Most people who come to Antarctica are scientists, but tourists are starting to visit the ice-covered land. They all share a love of adventure. In 2001, two brave adventurers, Ann Bancroft of the USA and Liv Arneson of Norway, became the first women to ski across the entire continent, pulling sleds the whole way!

1. Which words best describe Antarctica?
   - o a. sunny and bright
   - o b. rainy and muddy
   - ● c. ice-covered, cold, and windy
   - o d. land of lakes and rivers

2. What animal does not live in Antarctica?
   - o a. polar bear
   - o b. penguin
   - o c. seal
   - ● d. whale

3. What causes white out blizzards?
   - o a. severe snow storms
   - ● b. strong winds
   - o c. cloudy skies
   - o d. none of the above

4. Who are Ann Bancroft and Liv Arneson?
   - o a. scientists studying the South Pole
   - ◍ b. skiing adventurers
   - o c. mountain climbers
   - o d. women looking for fossils

5. When is the best time to visit Antarctica?
   - o a. during a white out
   - o b. in the winter
   - ◍ c. in the summer
   - o d. none of the above

6. Which of the following can you find in Antarctica?
   - o a. dolphins
   - o b. polar bears
   - ◍ c. South Pole
   - o d. North Pole

7. What happens during the summer in Antarctica?
   - o a. Scientists leave to go home.
   - o b. The wind never blows.
   - ◍ c. There is 24 hours of daylight.
   - o d. It rains all day long.

8. Most people who come to Antarctica are
   - o a. tourists.
   - o b. skiers.
   - o c. explorers.
   - ◍ d. scientists.

9. How fast can the wind blow in Antarctica?
   - ◍ a. 100 mph
   - o b. 30 mph
   - o c. 70 mph
   - o d. none of the above

ACTIVITY # 3

When you look at sand on the beach or in the desert, it may look plain and ordinary. But when you look at sand under a microscope, you will see that it comes in different sizes, shapes, and colors all over the world.

Sand mainly consists of grains of minerals that have been weathered out of rocks. In the desert, winds blow the grains around so that they keep bumping into each other. This gives the desert grains of sand a very round, uniform shape and size. In a river or ocean, sand grains do not collide with each other as often because the water acts as a kind of cushion. This means that grains of ocean sand and sand found in river bottoms do not have such a round shape.

Scientists have studied grains of sand for years. Looking at the kinds of minerals that make up the sand helps American scientists to locate diamonds. They know that certain minerals are often found near diamonds, so they know that if they find these minerals, diamonds are not far away!

1. The best title for this selection is _____.
   - o a. "Diamonds"
   - ● b. "Sand"
   - o c. "Ocean Sand"
   - o d. "Desert Sand"

2. A grain of river bottom sand is
   - o a. round.
   - o b. rounder than a grain of desert sand.
   - ● c. not as round as a grain of desert sand.
   - o d. the same as any other grain of sand.

3. What is sand mostly made of?
   - ● a. minerals
   - o b. water
   - o c. diamonds
   - o d. none of the above

4. What makes desert sand round-shaped?
   - o a. water
   - o b. dirt
   - o c. diamonds
   - ● d. wind

5. Grains of ocean sand are similar to

  o a. grains of desert sand.
  ● b. grains of river bottom sand.
  o c. diamonds.
  o d. none of the above

6. Weathered rocks are
  o a. brand new rocks.
  o b. only found in the ocean.
  o c. only found in the desert.
  ● d. broken up by wind, rain, and temperature changes.

7. Looking at the kinds of minerals in sand
  o a. is the work of park rangers.
  o b. is dirty business.
  ● c. helps people find diamonds.
  o d. is best done in the ocean.

8. Scientists who study sand use
  o a. sand paper.
  ● b. microscopes.
  o c. mirrors.
  o d. telescopes.

Practice Skill: COMPREHENSION OF RECREATIONAL SELECTIONS

Expectation: Read a story to understand a character's problem and how it is solved.

Tip: As you read a story, it is important to spot some important ideas. Here is what to look for.

<u>Characters and Setting</u>
Who is in the story?
What kind of personalities do they have?
Do their attitudes change throughout the story?
Where do they live?
Where does the story take place?

<u>Problem and Trying to Solve the Problem (The Plot)</u>
What happens to the characters?
What are the main events in the story?

<u>Resolution or Conclusion</u>
How is the problem solved?

As you discover these things about the story, think about other stories you have read that have similar or different plots and characters.

Read the following short story. Think about what you read. Then read the question and choose the best answer.

Jason and his sister, Megan, were walking home from school one day. They were almost home when they noticed they were being followed by a fluffy white dog with long hair and short, stubby legs. They stopped. He stopped. They walked. He walked, too. They talked. The little white dog barked.

"Who could he belong to?" wondered Megan. "Where did he come from?"

"He just showed up. He's not wearing a collar. Let's keep him," said Jason.

"No way, Jason. Mom will have a fit! Just keep on walking and don't look back," Megan warned.

"Ruff, ruff!" barked the little white dog. Jason was sure that he was saying, "Keep me."

"See? He wants to stay with us. He just said so," insisted Jason. Megan shook her head and started toward home again. The little white dog followed right behind them all the way home.

Their mother came out to greet them. Before she could say anything, the little white dog stopped in front of her and started to lick her toes. He looked up at her with his big blue eyes

"Can we keep him, Mom? Oh, please?" asked Jason.

"He must belong to someone, Jason. It wouldn't be fair to his owners. They would miss him."

Megan offered a solution. "What if we call the animal shelter and make posters about the lost dog that we found? Then if nobody calls, we can keep him. What do you say, Mom?"

The little white dog just kept licking Mother's toes and looking cuter with every lick. Finally, she just sighed and answered, "I know when I'm licked."

Jason and Megan got right to work on the posters. They put them up on every corner between school and home. They waited to see if anyone would call. No one called on the first day. No one called on the second day. On the third day, a little girl called to ask them if they had found her dog, Penny.

"She's a little white dog with long hair and short, stubby legs. She looks like a little mop sweeping the ground." Jason's heart sank. He really had wanted to keep the dog. "One more thing," said the voice on the phone. "She has a little black spot on the top of her head between her ears." Jason was so relieved he could hardly speak. There was no black spot on his dog's head.

"I'm sorry," he replied. "This is not Penny."

The next four days passed slowly for Megan and Jason, but no one else called about the dog. On the last day, their mother told them they could keep the little white dog. They named him Blizzard.

1. Where were Megan and Jason going?
   - o a. to school
   - o b. to a dog show
   - ⦾ c. home from school
   - o d. to the park

2. Which character in the story asks Mother for the dog?
   - o a. Megan
   - ⦾ b. Jason
   - o c. Mother
   - o d. the telephone caller

3. Why did Mother not want to keep the dog?
   - o a. It couldn't do any tricks.
   - o b. It was dirty.
   - ⦾ c. It might already belong to someone else.
   - o d. It was too little.

4. Who thinks of a plan to try to keep the dog?
   - ⦾ a. Megan
   - o b. Jason
   - o c. Mother
   - o d. none of the above

5. Who was Penny?
   - o a. a neighbor
   - o b. Jason's new dog
   - ⊙ c. the telephone caller's dog
   - o d. none of the above

6. How did Jason feel when he first heard the caller describe her lost dog?
   - o a. confused
   - o b. mad
   - ⊙ c. sad
   - o d. none of the above

7. How did Jason feel at the end of his conversation with the caller?
   - o a. confused
   - o b. mad
   - o c. sad
   - ⊙ d. none of the above

8. What did they name the little white dog?
   - o a. Mop
   - o b. Little White Dog
   - o c. Penny
   - ⊙ d. Blizzard

9. How were Penny and Blizzard different?
   - o a. Blizzard had a black spot on her head.
   - o b. One was black and one was white.
   - o c. One was larger than the other.
   - ⊙ d. Penny had a black spot on her head.

10. Which of the following statements is true?
   - o a. Megan and Jason wanted to keep the dog.
   - ⊙ b. Megan did not want to keep the dog.
   - o c. Father did not want to keep the dog.
   - o d. Penny wanted to stay with Blizzard.

Practice Skill: FUNCTIONAL READING

Expectation: Follow directions to perform a real-life task.

Tip: Sometimes you read to follow step-by-step directions. This is an important reason to read. When you read for this purpose, you must read every word carefully and think about the order of doing things.

Read the following selection. Choose the best answer to each question.

Make Your Own Pretzels

You can make your own pretzels at home with a little help from an adult. It's not very hard. Give it a go! First of all, get organized. Read the directions carefully. Make sure you have everything you need. Wash your hands, and you're ready to go!

Ingredients (What you need):
   1 package of dry, quick-rising yeast
   1 ½ Cups of warm water in a bowl
   1 Tablespoon sugar
   1 Teaspoon salt
   4 Cups all purpose flour
   1 large egg, beaten
   ¼ Cup course salt
Directions (What you do):
   1. Preheat oven to 425°.
   2. Dissolve the yeast in the bowl of warm water.
   3. Add sugar and salt to the water and yeast.
   4. Add the flour. Stir with a wooden spoon until it forms smooth dough.
   5. Knead the dough with your hands for 3 – 5 minutes. Sprinkle flour on the work surface so the dough won't stick.
   6. Break the dough into small pieces, about the size of golf balls.
   7. Roll each piece into a long snake. Twist the snake into a pretzel.
   8. Put the pretzels on a nonstick baking sheet.
   9. Brush the pretzels with beaten egg and sprinkle with course salt.
   10. Bake at 425° for 12-15 minutes, or until golden brown.

1. To make pretzels you will need
   - o   a. milk and eggs.
   - ⊚ b. flour and water.
   - o   c. mustard and sugar.
   - o   d. a snake.

2. What do you need that is not listed in the ingredients?
   - o   a. a bowl
   - o   b. a beaten egg
   - ⊚ c. a nonstick baking sheet and a wooden spoon
   - o   d. sugar

3. Before you preheat the oven, what should you do?
   - ⊚ a. get organized
   - o   b. break the dough into small pieces
   - o   c. beat the egg
   - o   d. none of the above

4. What helps to keep the dough from sticking to the work surface?
   - o   a. a wooden spoon
   - o   b. egg
   - ⊚ c. flour
   - o   d. none of the above

5. Which step comes first?
   - ⊚ a. knead the dough
   - o   b. make the golf balls
   - o   c. make a snake
   - o   d. make the pretzel shape

6. Which step comes last?
   - o   a. make the pretzel shape
   - o   b. preheat the oven
   - o   c. make the golf ball
   - ⊚ d. brush with egg and sprinkle with salt

7. What do you need that is not mentioned in the directions?
   - ⊚ a. a potholder
   - o   b. a baking sheet
   - o   c. a bowl
   - o   d. a wooden spoon

Practice Skill: CAUSE AND EFFECT

Expectation: Make inferences based on information the writer tells you and what you already know. Be able to tell what happened and why.

> Tip: In a story, a writer does not tell you everything. You must think about what she does tell you and make some educated guesses about other things. This is called "making inferences." You read what the writer says, and you use what you know from your own life to make sense of what you are reading.
>
> Look at this sentence: The player fell, and the other team scored. What happened is the effect (the team scored). After you know what happened, you may have to think why. Some sentences do not give the reason. You have to figure out from the clues what the cause was. These exercises will give you practice in identifying and making inferences.

Read each sentence. Choose the best answer.

1. It was cold outside, so
    o a. I put on my bathing suit.
    o b. I walked my dog.
    ⦿ c. I put on my jacket.
    o d. None of the above

2. I heard thunder, and then
    o a. the phone rang.
    o b. the ball bounced.
    ⦿ c. I saw the lightning.
    o d. None of the above

3. Eloy was happy because
    o a. he lost his cap.
    o b. he had a lot of homework.
    o c. he got lost.
    ⦿ d. None of the above

4. I hurried out the door
   - a. so I would be late.
   - b. so I wouldn't be late.
   - c. so I could finish my soup.
   - d. None of the above

5. I started walking to the kitchen
   - a. because I jumped rope.
   - b. so I could finish my soup.
   - c. because I have a cat.
   - d. None of the above

6. There were white lines in the sky.
   - a. The volcano was starting to erupt.
   - b. The test missile had been launched.
   - c. There would be extra dessert tonight.
   - d. I took my scissors out of the drawer.

7. Liliana laughed at my jokes and made me smile.
   - a. Liliana was a sad person.
   - b. Liliana was a good friend.
   - c. Liliana could ride a bike.
   - d. Liliana has many toys.

8. Mo sat in the dirt for a minute before he dusted himself off. Then he got right back on again.
   - a. Mo was in the bathtub.
   - b. Mo was reading a book in bed.
   - c. Mo was riding a horse.
   - d. Mo was eating his lunch.

It was a hot day. Susana had been playing basketball with her friends.
   "May we have a drink of water, Mom?" asked Susana.
   "Sure," she replied. "The cups are in the cupboard."

9. Which is the best inference to make?
   - a. Susana's mother is not home.
   - b. Susana will not get her friends a drink.
   - c. Susana and her friends are thirsty.
   - d. Susana and her friends are hungry.

Damon heard the rooster crow. It was time to get up and help Uncle Joe milk the cow and feed the horses.

10. Which is the best inference to make?
   o a. Damon has many pets.
   o b. Damon lives in the city.
   ø c. Uncle Joe lives on a farm.
   o d. The horses won't eat hay.

Simon pulled his sleeping bag around him. He stared up at the stars in the sky. There must be a million of them. The campfire was glowing.

11. What is the best inference to make?
   o a. Simon is standing on the roof.
   ø b. The story takes place at night in a campground.
   o c. Simon is afraid.
   o d. It was a stormy night.

Jamila was waiting for the start buzzer. Her heart was pounding. In a moment she would hear the splash and feel the cool water all around her. She wondered if the other competitors were feeling the same way.

12. What is the best inference to make?
   o a. Jamila is a marathon runner.
   o b. Jamila read the newspaper.
   ø c. Jamila is a swimmer.
   o d. Jamila in an ice skater.

13. What is the best inference to make?
   ø a. Jamila is excited.
   o b. Jamila is tired.
   o c. Jamila will run away.
   o d. Jamila forgot her shoes.

Practice Skill: READING VOCABULARY

Expectation: Identify synonyms – words that mean the same or nearly the same thing.

Tip: Knowing many synonyms for words will make your writing more interesting and will help you explain exactly what you mean. For example, instead of big house, you might use villa, mansion, estate, or castle. Each one brings a different picture to the reader's mind.

Decide which word means nearly the same as the <u>underlined</u> word. Choose the best answer.

1. a <u>weary</u> traveler
   - o a. sure-footed
   - ◉ b. tired
   - o c. dirty
   - o d. none of the above

2. <u>skim</u> the newspaper article
   - ◉ a. scan
   - o b. opinion
   - o c. touch
   - o d. none of the above

3. <u>capture</u> the thief
   - o a. watch
   - o b. punish
   - ◉ c. catch
   - o d. none of the above

4. <u>adore</u> my grandfather
   - o a. fight
   - o b. miss
   - ◉ c. love
   - o d. none of the above

5. drive your <u>vehicle</u>

    ● a. car
    o b. pilot
    o c. cruise
    o d. none of the above

6. <u>supportive </u>friends

    o a. hurtful
    ● b. helpful
    o c. wandering
    o d. none of the above

7. <u>voyage</u> overseas

    o a. bridge
    o b. journey
    ● c. ship
    o d. none of the above

8. a <u>unique</u> gift shop

    o a. jewelry
    o b. expensive
    ● c. one of a kind
    o d. none of the above

9. <u>divide</u> the winnings

    ● a. split
    o b. organize
    o c. destroy
    o d. none of the above

10. a mountain <u>village</u>

    o a. tower
    ● b. town
    o c. stream
    o d. none of the above

Practice Skill: CAPITALIZATION

Expectation: Recognize errors in capitalization.

Tip: Use capital letters to begin a sentence; for days of the week, holidays, months; for proper names of people and places; and for the first word of a direct quotation.

Read lines a, b, and c together. Pay attention to capitalization. Then choose the line that has a mistake in capitalization. If there are no mistakes, select choice "d. All are correct."

1. ○ a. my sister told me
   ○ b. to be careful. Of
   ○ c. course, I am always careful.
   ○ d. All are correct.

2. ○ a. The fourth of july
   ○ b. is fun because
   ○ c. of the fireworks.
   ○ d. All are correct.

3. ○ a. Susan told me
   ○ b. that sara and i
   ○ c. could play with her.
   ○ d. All are correct.

4. ○ a. My mother's favorite
   ○ b. fairy tale character
   ○ c. is cinderella.
   ○ d. All are correct.

5. ○ a. We took an airplane
   ○ a. to visit our grandparents
   ○ b. in california.
   ○ c. All are correct.

1. o a. My father warned me,
   o b. "be sure to take your coat.
   o c. The storm is coming."
   ⊙ d. All are correct.

2. o a. My favorite day
   ⊙ b. of the week is saturday
   o c. because I get to sleep late.
   o d. All are correct.

3. o a. I told aunt Betty
   o b. that I thought her
   o c. locket was pretty.
   ⊙ d. All are correct.

4. o a. This year we will
   ⊙ b. study the Rivers and Mountains
   o c. in North America.
   o d. All are correct.

5. o a. I told her that
   ⊙ b. She had the prettiest
   o c. eyes I ever saw.
   o d. All are correct.

6. ⊙ a. The Lawyer told
   o b. me to go to law school
   o c. when I grow up.
   o d. All are correct.

7. o a. At the beginning of
   o b. every sporting event in the United States,
   o c. we stand to hear "The Star Spangled Banner."
   ⊙ d. All are correct.

Practice Skill: PUNCTUATION

Expectation: Correctly use periods, question marks, exclamation points, and commas in sentences.

```
Tip:
Use a period:
    • to end a statement.
    • after an abbreviation such as Dr. or Mrs.
Use a question mark:
    • to end a question.
Use an exclamation point:
    •   after a word, phrase, or sentence that shows strong
feeling.
Use a comma:
    • after each word in a series of three or more.
    • after a city name if the state follows.
    • after a greeting of a letter.
    • after the closing of a letter.
    • in dates, after the day of the month and before the year.
```

Read lines a, b, and c together. Pay attention to punctuation. Then choose the line that has a mistake in punctuation. If there are no mistakes, select choice "d. All are correct."

1. a. Mary John Sue Bill and Tom
    o b. are going to Miami,
    o c. Florida.
    o d. All are correct.

2. o a. What do you
    b. want to do today.
    o c. I am bored.
    o d. All are correct.

1. o a . Yikes! What
   ø b. a big dog?
   o c. What's his name?
   o d. All are correct.

2. ø a. June 30 2001
   o b. Dear Grandma and Grandpa,
   o c. Please come to visit us soon.
   o d. All are correct.

3. o a. My mom put
   o b. a sandwich hard apple cookie napkin
   o c. and drink in my lunch.
   ø d. All are correct.

4. o a. My dentist's name
   o b. is Dr Good. He
   o c. is a kind man.
   ø d. All are correct.

5. o a. The horse galloped away,
   o b. and the frightened rider
   ø c. yelled, "Whoa, boy. Help me. Yikes."
   o d. All are correct.

6. o a. "Mom, will you please
   o b. take me to Disneyland
   o c. for my birthday." I asked.
   ø d. All are correct.

7. o a. I can't believe
   ø b. it? I won
   o c. the poetry contest!
   o d. all are correct.

8. o a. "Wow! Could
   o b. she be my long
   o c. lost cat?" wondered John.
   ø d. All are correct.

Practice Skill: WORD USAGE

Expectation: Use words correctly in sentences.

Tip: When you do each of these exercises, read the sentence and say "Mmmmm" when you come to the blank. Then read the sentence again, but this time substitute the first word choice for the "Mmmmm." Do this until you have substituted each word choice for the blank in the sentence. Listen to the sound of each sentence. This will help you eliminate many choices.

Try each answer choice in the blank. Choose the word or words that best fit in the sentence.

1. One twin is __*shorter*__ than the other.
   - o a. short
   - Ⓞ b. shorter
   - o c. shortest
   - o d. none of the above

2. I bought a pair of __*socks*__ at the store.
   - Ⓞ a. socks
   - o b. sock
   - o c. sockses
   - o d. none of the above

3. Ben __*took*__ his books to school.
   - o a. take
   - o b. taked
   - Ⓞ c. took
   - o d. none of the above

4. We __*spent*__ all our money on toys.
   - Ⓞ a. spent
   - o b. spends
   - o c. spended
   - o d. none of the above

5. Mr. Palmer _____carefully_____ went up the stairs.

   - a. careful
   - b. carefulness
   - c. carefully
   - d. none of the above

6. The swing _____Was twisting_____ in the breeze.

   - a. was twisting
   - b. were twisting
   - c. twisting
   - d. none of the above

7. I _____barely_____ understood what he was saying.

   - a. bared
   - b. bare
   - c. barely
   - d. none of the above

8. He _____ in the lake.

   - a. swim
   - b. swimming
   - c. swimmed
   - d. none of the above

9. The baby _____cried_____ all night long.

   - a. cry
   - b. cried
   - c. crying
   - d. none of the above

10. We _____brought_____ our dog to the park.

   - a. bringed
   - b. brung
   - c. brought
   - d. none of the above

Practice Skills : SENTENCE STRUCTURE AND
CONTENT ORGANIZATION

Expectation: Recognize correct sentence organization
and structure.

Tip: Good writers organize their thoughts and write them down
clearly to make it easy for their readers to understand. They
think about the sequence of events (what happens first, next, and
last). They make a list, an outline, or a map of what they want to
write. After they write a first draft, they edit it to make it as
clear as it can be.

As you do the following exercises, think about what the
writer is trying to say. Edit the sentences to make them clearer.

**Read the sentences. Then read the choices to see if one of them
expresses the thought in a better way. If none of the choices is better
than the original sentence, choose "d. No change."**

1. Tom took a walk. Across the street. He walked carefully.

   o a. Tom carefully walked. Across the street carefully.
   o b. Carefully walked across the street went Tom.
   ⊗ c. Tom carefully walked across the street.
   o d. No change.

2. Looking for the fireworks last year. That's what we did when we took a
   wrong turn and we got lost that last Fourth of July last year.

   o a. That last Fourth of July, we got lost last year. And we took a
         wrong turn last time. And we got lost last time. The fireworks
         was what we were looking for last year.
   o b. Last year we got lost. Last year we looked for fireworks. Last
         year we got lost. Last year we took a wrong turn. Last year on
         Fourth of July.
   ⊚ c. Last year on the Fourth of July, while we were looking for
         fireworks, we took a wrong turn and got lost.
   o d. No change.

Grade 2 Edition   41

3. We went to the lake, we went swimming, we had a picnic, we stayed out late.

   o a. We went to the lake and we went swimming and we had a picnic, and we stayed out late.
   o b. We went to the lake. We went swimming. We had a picnic. We stayed out late.
   ● c. When we went to the lake, we swam, had a picnic, and stayed out late.
   o d. No change.

4. At the amusement park, we rode on the roller coaster, the hammer ride, the bumper cars, and the sky buckets.

   o a. We rode on the roller coaster, and we rode on the hammer ride, and we rode on a lot of stuff.
   o b. A roller coaster, and a hammer ride, and a sky bucket ride, and a bumper car ride. That's what we rode on at the amusement park.
   o c. The amusement park rides were where we were going to ride the bumper cars and the sky buckets, the roller coasters and the hammer rides, etc.
   ● d. No change.

5. She walked to school, ate her breakfast, woke up, got out of bed, and gave her dad a hug goodbye.

   o a. She walked to school. She ate her breakfast. She woke up. She got out of bed. And she gave her dad a goodbye hug.
   o b. After she walked to school, she ate her breakfast, she woke up, got out of bed, and gave her dad a goodbye hug.
   ● c. After she woke up and got out of bed, she ate her breakfast, gave her dad a goodbye hug, and walked to school.
   o d. No change.

6. Every year our school has a country fair. It is great fun for everyone. There are pony rides, sack races, a water balloon toss, and a parade. One of the most popular events is when the principal sits in the dunking booth. Everyone tries to get her wet!

o a. Our country fair happens every year. It's really fun. Everyone tries to get the principal all wet. There's the dunking booth part and there's the pony rides and the sack races and the parade part of the country fair. It's really fun. The parents and the kids really have fun.

o b. We have a country fair at our school every year. We have pony rides. We have sack races. We have a parade. We have a water balloon toss. We have lots of fun. We have a dunking booth. We all try to get the principal wet. We have lots of fun.

o c. Country fair. At our school we have one. Every year it's good. It's really fun. They have pony rides, sack races, water balloons tossings, parade. They put our principal in the dunking booth. She get wet. It's the really fun thing that everybody likes. The whole fair is really fun.

● d. No change.

7. We took the train to San Diego. We got up early. We got really wet in the water. We went to the beach. Lots of waves. We took the train back home the next day. We stayed over night. It made us tired. All the things we did. We saw all the marine life in the tide pools.

o a. We took the train and stayed overnight in San Diego. All the things we did made us tired like waves and tide pools.

o b. We got up early to go to San Diego. Took the train to the beach. Took it back home again. Stayed overnight. We were tired. We did so many things. Including tide pools and beach.

● c. We took the train to San Diego. We did many fun things there. We went to the beach, got wet playing in the waves, and saw marine life in the tide pools. We were so tired after such a full day that we stayed overnight and took the train home the next day.

o d. No change.

Practice Skills: STUDY SKILLS

Expectation: Use alphabetizing skills to locate information.

Tip: It is important to know how to alphabetize words (put them in A-B-C order) and how to find a particular word in an alphabetized list. Why is this so? Most resource books contain thousands of facts, and they are written so that you do not have to read them from start to finish. Very few people read an entire encyclopedia or dictionary! Because those books are organized in alphabetical order, it is easy to find information in them. Many other books have an index (an alphabetical list of topics that are contained in the book and the pages where you can read about that topic). The exercises in this section will help you apply your alphabetizing skills so that you can be a fast researcher.

Read the question and choose the best answer.

1. Which word comes first in alphabetical order?
   - o a. made
   - o b. mist
   - ⦿ c. carry
   - o d. dog

2. Which word comes first in alphabetical order?
   - o a. Animals
   - o b. Reptiles
   - o c. Mammals
   - ⦿ d. Amphibians

3. Which word comes first in alphabetical order?
   - o a. whose
   - o b. wish
   - ⦿ c. whisper
   - o d. whispering

4. Which word comes first in alphabetical order?

   ϕ a. man
   ϕ b. mane
   o c. map
   o d. master

5. Which word comes first in alphabetical order?

   o a. Jones
   o b. Johnson
   ϕ c. James
   o d. Jenkins

If your dictionary is divided into 2 volumes, with volume 1 covering A-K and volume 2 covering L-Z, which volume would contain each of the following words?

6. minute
   o a. volume 1
   ϕ b. volume 2

7. organize
   o a. volume 1
   ϕ b. volume 2

8. cartoon
   ϕ a. volume 1
   o b. volume 2

9. wonder
   o a. volume 1
   ϕ b. volume 2

10. horse
   ϕ a. volume 1
   o b. volume 2

11. kerchief
   ϕ a. volume 1
   o b. volume 2

12. licorice
   o a. volume 1
   ϕ b. volume 2

If you have a single volume dictionary, in what part would you find the following words?

11. bear

    ● a. towards the beginning
    o b. in the middle
    o c. towards the end

12. notice

    o a. towards the beginning
    ● b. in the middle
    o c. towards the end

15. whisper

    o a. towards the beginning
    o b. in the middle
    ● c. towards the end

16. In a dictionary, which word would you find between *carrot* and *elephant?*

    ● a. curl
    o b. camel
    o c. girl
    o d. exercise

17. In a dictionary, which word would you find between *smart* and *stretch?*

    o a. slim
    o b. suffer
    o c. strong
    ● d. solar

Use this index from a resource book to answer each question. Choose the best answer.

African Elephant	2
Asian Elephant	3
Alligator	25, 28
-Difference from Crocodile	28
Arctic Land Animals	12, 15
Bear	10, 12, 13
Crocodile	27, 28
-Difference from Alligator	28
Grizzly Bear	10, 13
Koala	45
Polar Bear	12
Rattlesnake	51
Seal	15
Snake	50-55

18. What is the subject of the book?
   - a. Africa
   - b. Arctic Animals
   - c. Animals
   - d. Birds

19. To read about snakes in general, you would go to page(s) _____.
   - a. 50 – 55
   - b. 49
   - c. 50
   - d. 51

20. To read about rattlesnakes in particular, you would go to page(s) _____.
   - a. 25
   - b. 51
   - c. 50-55
   - d. 15

21. From the index, you can tell that
   - a. a koala is not a bear.
   - b. there is no difference between an alligator and a crocodile.
   - c. the book does not contain information about snakes.
   - d. there are no animals in the Arctic.

Practice Skill: CONTRACTIONS

Expectation: Identify and make contractions.

Tip: A contraction is two words joined together with one or more letters dropped and replaced by an apostrophe ('). (Do not = don't, I will = I'll). If you are having trouble with contractions, try using them in a sentence. For example, say to yourself, "I will not be afraid." Then think of another way to say the same thing using a contraction: "I won't be afraid." It works! The contraction for "will not" is "won't."

ACTIVITY # 1

1. Write the contraction for each word.

    a. you are ___you're___   we are ___we're___

    b. she is ___she's___   there is ___there's___

    c. he will ___he'll___   cannot ___can't___

    d. you will ___you'll___   they are ___they're___

2. Underline the contraction in each sentence below.

    a. We wanted him to come over, but he <u>can't</u>.

    b. She <u>doesn't</u> understand why her friend will not go.

    c. <u>Won't</u> you please help me check my homework?

    d. <u>Isn't</u> that a furry cat?

3. Draw a line to match each pair of words with its contraction.

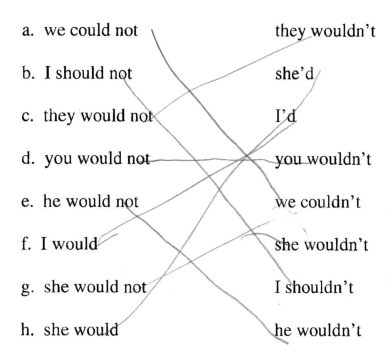

a. we could not   they wouldn't

b. I should not   she'd

c. they would not   I'd

d. you would not   you wouldn't

e. he would not   we couldn't

f. I would   she wouldn't

g. she would not   I shouldn't

h. she would   he wouldn't

4. Underline 1 or more contractions in each sentence below.

a. Isn't it true that her aunt's cat had kittens?

b. They're going to sleep at their neighbor's house.

c. It's going to help if there's a cool pool at their house.

d. I can't tell if it's going to rain.

e. The dog wagged its tail as if to say, "Where's my bone?"

ACTIVITY # 2   Choose the correct contraction for each pair of words.

1. we are
   - o a. were
   - o b. we'd
   - o c. we'll
   - ⊚ d. we're

2. will not
   - o a. willn't
   - ⊚ b. won't
   - o c. we've
   - o d. will

3. I would
   - ⊚ a. I'd
   - o b. I wouldn't
   - o c. I'll
   - o d. I'ld

4. does not
   - o a. don't
   - ⊚ b. doesn't
   - o c. didn't
   - o d. do'nt

5. do not
   - ⊚ a. don't
   - o b. doesn't
   - o c. didn't
   - o d. do'nt

6. did not
   - o a. don't
   - o b. doesn't
   - ⊚ c. didn't
   - o d. did'nt

7. you will
   - o a. you won't
   - o b. you wil'
   - ⊚ c. you'll
   - o d. you willn't

Practice Skills: SPELLING

Expectation: Correctly spell frequently used words and irregular words such as *was, were, says, said, who, what, why.* Correctly spell words with basic short-vowel long-vowel, r-controlled, and consonant-blend patterns.

Tip: Many words are spelled exactly the way they sound. There are other words that follow a pattern. The others need to be learned by memorizing the sequence of the letters. As you do these exercises, think about whether the word follows a spelling rule, is spelled like it sounds, or whether it is one that you just have to memorize.

SPELLING ACTIVITY # 1

You can see many interesting things at the zoo. Unscramble each word to find a zoo animal.

1. reba   ___bear___

2. xof   ___fox___

3. niol   ___lion___

4. okala   ___koala___

5. riget   ___tiger___

6. phelante   ___elephant___

7. lalitagro   ___alligator___

8. ekans   ___snake___

9. chostri   ___ostrich___

10. effirga   ___giraffe___

SPELLING ACTIVITY # 2

Put each group of words in alphabetical order.

fast	_famous_	many	_man_
first	_fast_	man	_manners_
famous	_file_	manners	_many_
file	_first_	map	_map_

brick	_brain_	crust	_cracker_
brain	_brick_	cracker	_critter_
brought	_brother_	crow	_crow_
brother	_broght_	critter	_crust_

SPELLING ACTIVITY # 3

Rearrange the <u>underlined</u> letters of each word so it fits the clue for the new word you spelled.

1. <u>mate</u> -- not wild _tame_

2. <u>tea</u> -- what we do at meals _eat_

3. <u>meat</u> – players of a game who have the same goal _team_

4. <u>won</u> – at this moment _now_

5. <u>not</u> -- two thousand pounds _ton_

SPELLING ACTIVITY # 4 – NOUN PLURALS (more than one)

Add <u>s</u>, <u>es</u>, or <u>ies</u> to the following words to make them plural words.

dish _dishs_

tray _trays_

box _boxes_

watch _watches_

sock _socks_

plate _plates_

word _words_

party _palties_

horse _horses_

taxi _taxis_

puppy _puppies_

boy _boys_

movie _movies_

lunch _lunchs_

candy _candies_

berry _berries_

SPELLING ACTIVITY # 5

**Read each group of words. Mark the one that is <u>not</u> spelled correctly.
If all the words are spelled correctly, choose answer "d. no mistake."**

1. o a. have
    ◉ b. frum
    o c. the
    o d. no mistake

2. o a. said
    o b. one
    o c. and
    ◉ d. no mistake

3. o a. once
    ◉ b. wonse
    o c. from
    o d. no mistake

4. ◉ a. whith
    o b. with
    o c. we
    o d. no mistake

5. o a. come
    o b. card
    o c. came
    ◉ d. no mistake

6. o a. you
    o b. not
    ◉ c. thay
    o d. no mistake

7. ◉ a. siad
    o b. said
    o c. say
    o d. no mistake

8.　○　a.　they
　　○　b.　them
　　○　c.　over
　　◉　d.　no mistake

9.　◉　a.　meny
　　○　b.　man
　　○　c.　men
　　○　d.　no mistake

10.○　a.　words
　　◉　b.　frist
　　○　c.　first
　　○　d.　bird

11.○　a.　just
　　○　b.　who
　　◉　c.　doun
　　○　d.　no mistake

12.◉　a.　calld
　　○　b.　most
　　○　c.　only
　　○　d.　no mistake

13.◉　a.　eech
　　○　b.　been
　　○　c.　free
　　○　d.　no mistake

14.○　a.　very
　　○　b.　many
　　◉　c.　undr
　　○　d.　no mistake

15.○　a.　where
　　○　b.　were
　　○　c.　what
　　◉　d.　no mistake

16. o a. coud
    o b. cold
    o c. could
    o d. no mistake

17. o a. purple
    o b. pensul
    o c. paper
    o d. no mistake

18. o a. appel
    o b. apple
    o c. grape
    o d. no mistake

19. o a. famly
    o b. family
    o c. forest
    o d. no mistake

20. o a. women
    o b. woman
    o c. watch
    o d. no mistake

21. o a. clock
    o b. listen
    o c. littel
    o d. no mistake

22. o a. door
    o b. pack
    o c. water
    o d. no mistake

SPELLING ACTIVITY # 6

Find the word that best fits the sentence and is spelled correctly.

1. My arm _____ .
   - o a. hurts
   - o b. hirts
   - o c. herts
   - o d. none of the above

2. She went the _____ way.
   - o a. othr
   - o b. uther
   - o c. other
   - o d. none of the above

3. _____ you like to go to the movies?
   - o a. Wood
   - o b. Wud
   - o c. Would
   - o d. none of the above

4. How many _____ came to your party?
   - o a. peepul
   - o b. people
   - o c. peaple
   - o d. none of the above

5. I ate _____ I was hungry.
   - o a. becuse
   - o b. becuse
   - o c. because
   - o d. none of the above

6. _____ are my shoes?
   - o a. Whear
   - o b. Wear
   - o c. Were
   - o d. none of the above

SPELLING ACTIVITY # 7

Read the sentences. Look for the word with the spelling mistake.

1. She dranck a glass of ice cold water.
   - a. dranck
   - o b. glass
   - o c. ice
   - o d. water

2. She thought abowt what she said.
   - o a. thought
   - b. abowt
   - o c. what
   - o d. said

3. He dosn't understand the math problem.
   - a. dosn't
   - o b. understand
   - o c. math
   - o d. problem

4. Ann's mother called her to dinner agin.
   - o a. mother
   - o b. called
   - o c. dinner
   - d. agin

5. I herd a strange noise outdoors.
   - a. herd
   - o b. strange
   - o c. noise
   - o d. outdoors

6. My aunt is older then my mother.
   - o a. aunt
   - o b. older
   - c. then
   - o d. mother

SPELLING ACTIVITY # 8

Find the word that best fits the sentence and is spelled correctly.

1. I am a ___very___ good student.
   - ⊘ a. very
   - o b. vary
   - o c. verry
   - o d. vurry

2. How ___many___ fish did you catch?
   - o a. meny
   - o b. menny
   - ⊙ c. many
   - o d. manny

3. We ___were___ running down the street.
   - o a. where
   - ⊙ b. were
   - o c. wer
   - o d. wher

4. My father read the ___sign___ above the door.
   - o a. sine
   - o b. sin
   - o c. sign
   - o d. signe

5. Will you ___please___ come to my party?
   - ⊙ a. please
   - o b. pleese
   - o c. pleeze
   - o d. pleas

6. The ___babies___ started crying.
   - o a. babys
   - o b. babbies
   - o c. babis
   - ⊙ d. babies

7. After _____School_____ I like to eat a snack.
   - o a. scool
   - o b. skool
   - o c. schol
   - ⊙ d. school

8. I _____really_____ like the present you gave me.
   - o a. realy
   - o b. reely
   - o c. reelly
   - o d. really

9. It was a _____ treat.
   - o a. speshul
   - ⊙ b. special
   - o c. specal
   - o d. speshal

10. He _____ a toy at the store.
   - o a. bot
   - o b. boght
   - ⊙ c. bought
   - o d. bouht

11. They gave their teacher a _____.
   - o a. suprise
   - o b. supprise
   - ⊙ c. surprise
   - o d. surprize

12. My aunt took a _____ of me.
   - o a. pitchur
   - ⊙ b. picture
   - o c. pichure
   - o d. pitcher

13. We _____ do our homework.
   - o a. all ways
   - o b. allways
   - o c. al ways
   - ⊙ d. always

Practice Skill: CAPITALIZATION

Expectation: Recognize correct and incorrect capitalization.

Tip: Be sure to capitalize all proper nouns (names of people, and names of particular places and things); the first word of a sentence or direct quotation; greeting and closing of letters; months of the year; days of the week; and titles and initials of people.

Read the sentences. Circle the capitalization mistakes. Can you find all of them? Check your answers below.

1. i Go to paradise valley school in nevada.
2. mrs. james is the Name of my Teacher.
3. WE are the Home of the paradise Valley panthers.
4. We will have a Carnival on the fourth SunDay in may.
5. One of the players for the las vegas wildcats will be there.
    Corrected Sentences
    1. I go to Paradise Valley School in Nevada.
    2. Mrs. James is the name of my teacher.
    3. We are the home of the Paradise Valley Panthers.
    4. We will have a carnival on the fourth Sunday in May.
    5. One of the players for the Las Vegas Wildcats will be there.

Choose the sentence that shows correct capitalization.

1. We do not go to school on _____.
    ● a. Sunday night
    o b. sunday night
    o c. Sunday Night
    o d. None of the above.

2. _____ is one of my favorite movies.
    o a. The little Mermaid
    o b. The little mermaid
    ● c. The Little Mermaid
    o d. None of the above

3. Our principal's name is _____ .
    o a. dr. marian Jones.
    o b. dr. Marian Jones
    ● c. Dr. Marian Jones
    o d. None of the above

4. I go to a fun _____ every summer.
    ● a. day camp
    o b. Day Camp
    o c. day Camp
    o d. None of the above

5. Have you ever read a book written by _____?
    o a. Dr Seuss
    o b. doctor Seuss
    ● c. Dr. Seuss
    o d. None of the above

6. I always sign my letters, _____.
    o a. your friend, Sylvia
    o b. Your Friend, Sylvia
    ● c. Your friend, Sylvia
    o d. None of the above

7. "_____" he politely asked.
    o a. what is the date today?
    o b. What is the Date today?
    o c. What is the date Today?
    ● d. None of the above

Capitalization – Activity # 2
In each exercise, find the sentence that has correct capitalization.

1. o a. How many toys do you have?
   o b. Can i ever come to your House?
   o c. On my Birthday we will go to grandma's house.
   o d. I will spend vacation at our favorite Beach.

2. o a. Let's play some Football.
   o b. My Friend said, "let's go to the park."
   o c. Once upon a Time, There was a lost cat.
   o d. We studied about Columbus and the Niña, Pinta, and Santa Maria.

3. o a. "Hi, mom. Where's dessert?" asked Ji Young.
   o b. I don't know the Song that's playing on the Radio.
   o c. Can i please have a bite of apple pie?
   o d. What is your favorite color?

4. o a. On Friday I have a Dentist's appointment.
   o b. On thursdays our parents visit school.
   o c. Next Saturday we will meet Uncle Joe at the airport.
   o d. My Doctor lives across the Street from us.

5. o a. Have you ever heard the song surfin usa?
   o b. We live in the United States of America.
   o c. Do you like Hot Dogs or Hamburgers?
   o d. The colors of our flag are Red, White, and Blue.

6. o a. "Hello, Mrs. cameron," said Janet.
   o b. It is usually very hot in August.
   o c. After it rains, Look for lots of mud puddles.
   o d. Have you ever listened to the beatles' music?

7. o a. We live near Two Strike Park.
   o b. We enjoy drinking Lemonade in the Ball Park.
   o c. What's dr. Lew's first name?
   o d. She signed the letter, "sincerely, Mona."

8. o a. John, kara, and i play softball together.
   o b. We will move from los angeles to boston.
   o c. I live on 187th street in portland.
   o d. In November, we celebrate Thanksgiving.

Practice Skill: SYNONYMS

Expectation: Identify words that have the same meaning.
Recognize words with multiple meanings.

Tip: As you do the following exercises, picture each one in your
mind to help you find the word that is the most similar to the
underlined word.   Think about the way the underlined word is
used in the particular phrase.   Remember that many words have
multiple meanings; they can mean different things in different
contexts.   For example, the word free has two very different
meanings in these two sentences:
(1) We won a free trip to San Diego.
(2) We took care of the hurt bird, and then set him free.
 In the first sentence, free means "costs nothing," while in the
second sentence it means "return to the wild."

**Read each item carefully. Find the word that means the same or almost
the same as the underlined word.**

1. The teacher thought he was a bright student.
    o a. careful
    o b. smart
    o c. silly
    o d. silent

2. They watched the miniature pony pull a cart.
    o a. fast
    o b. slow
    o c. tiny
    o d. huge

3. The lawyer wrote a speedy reply.
    o a. soft
    o b. special
    o c. quick
    o d. deep

4. The student gave a quick <u>reply</u>.
   - o a. answer
   - o b. horse
   - o c. car
   - o d. rest

5. A good friend can be the <u>key</u> to happiness.
   - o a. doorknob
   - o b. safe
   - o c. lock
   - o d. solution

6. It takes time to <u>heal</u> a broken bone.
   - o a. foot
   - o b. mend
   - o c. heat
   - o d. sole

7. Putting a new roof on a house is a difficult <u>task</u>.
   - o a. job
   - o b. house
   - o c. question
   - o d. time

8. We always try to think of a <u>brilliant</u> idea.
   - o a. cruel
   - o b. great
   - o c. confusing
   - o d. pet

9. There is no way that I could eat the <u>entire</u> pie.
   - o a. whole
   - o b. round
   - o c. messy
   - o d. delicious

10. In fairy tales, one of the characters is often a wild <u>beast</u>.
    - o a. ride
    - o b. job
    - o c. animal
    - o d. dream

11. After I lost the contest, my aunt had some <u>tender</u> words for me.
   - o a. tough
   - o b. caring
   - o c. chewy
   - o d. testy

12. This winter the temperature remained very <u>stable</u>.
   - o a. barn
   - o b. strong
   - o c. cold
   - o d. unchanged

Practice Skill: ANTONYMS

Expectation: Identify words with opposite meanings.

Tip: In these exercises you will think about antonyms. Antonyms are words that mean the opposite or nearly the opposite of each other. Think of a word that is very different from the underlined word.

Read each item carefully. Find the antonym of the underlined word.

1. Sung threw the ball <u>over</u> the fence.
   - o a. above
   - o b. near
   - o c. under
   - o d. with

2. Rembrandt is a very <u>famous</u> artist.
   - o a. blind
   - o b. unknown
   - o c. accomplished
   - o d. old

3. A good friend will often speak <u>kind</u> words.
   - o a. mean
   - o b. nice
   - o c. loud
   - o d. different

4. <u>quiet</u> voices
   - o a. peaceful
   - o b. private
   - o c. musical
   - o d. loud

5. a <u>cheap</u> toy
   - o a. birthday
   - o b. expensive
   - o c. broken
   - o d. large

6. a <u>giant</u> soda
   - o a. huge
   - o b. tiny
   - o c. gentle
   - o d. sparkling

7. <u>severe</u> punishment
   - o a. weak
   - o b. strong
   - o c. mean
   - o d. school

8. a <u>thick</u> rope
   - o a. thin
   - o b. strong
   - o c. twisted
   - o d. ship

9. a <u>calm</u> sea
   - o a. nervous
   - o b. stormy
   - o c. steady
   - o d. flat

10. a <u>calm</u> person
    - o a. nervous
    - o b. brave
    - o c. hungry
    - o d. serious

11. <u>fresh</u> bread
    - o a. delicious
    - o b. warm
    - o c. wheat
    - o d. stale

12. the <u>fancy</u> hat
    - o a. decorated
    - o b. bonnet
    - o c. plain
    - o d. ugly

Practice Skills: WORD ANALYSIS

Expectation: Identify words with the same sounds.

Tip: Good readers know that words are made of letters and that the letters stand for the sounds we make when we speak. They often read words by "sounding out" each letter or chunks of letters in the words. They also spot small words within larger words. The exercises below will help you practice these skills.

ACTIVITY # 1

Which small word or word chunk is <u>not</u> found in the given word?

1. yesterday
   o a. yes
   o b. day
   o c. er
   o d. at

2. understand
   o a. under
   o b. stand
   o c. un
   o d. sit

3. combination
   o a. tion
   o b. ber
   o c. com
   o d. bin

4. unspeakable
   o a. un
   o b. speak
   o c. under
   o d. able

5. fisherman
   o a. show   o c. ish
   o b. man   o d. isher

ACTIVITY # 2

Read the given word.   Emphasize the underlined sound. Then read the choices below and find another word that has the same <u>sound</u> as the underlined part.

1. b<u>ou</u>nce
   - o a. found
   - o b. grow
   - o c. prove
   - o d. through

2. c<u>ow</u>
   - o a. flow
   - o b. how
   - o c. grow
   - o d. below

3. f<u>ee</u>l
   - o a. fell
   - o b. keep
   - o c. feather
   - o d. felt

4. br<u>ea</u>kfast
   - o a. dream
   - o b. stream
   - o c. instead
   - o d. speak

5. afr<u>ai</u>d
   - o a. mail
   - o b. said
   - o c. Africa
   - o d. after

6. r<u>ea</u>dy
   - o a. dreamer
   - o b. clean
   - o c. reach
   - o d. weather

7. fr<u>o</u>g
   - o a. huge
   - o b. flag
   - o c. danger
   - o d. giraffe

ACTIVITY # 3

Find another real word in the given word.

1. battery
    - o a. tree
    - o b. batt
    - o c. bat
    - o d. ter

2. hospital
    - o a. spit
    - o b. tal
    - o c. hos
    - o d. hose

3. speculate
    - o a. special
    - o b. late
    - o c. cut
    - o d. pickle

4. organization
    - o a. niz
    - o b. organ
    - o c. tion
    - o d. iz

5. contraption
    - o a. tion
    - o b. cont
    - o c. ont
    - o d. trap

6. adjustment
    - o a. just
    - o b. mental
    - o c. judge
    - o d. statement

ANSWER KEY - LANGUAGE ARTS

<u>Reading Comprehension</u>

Practice Activity 1
1. B
2. A
3. B

Practice Activity 2
4. D
5. C
6. C

Activity 1
1. C
2. D
3. B
4. D
5. D

Activity 2
1. B
2. A
3. C
4. A
5. B

Activity 3
1. A
2. C
3. D
4. C
5. C

Activity 4
1. B
2. C
3. C
4. B
5. D

Activity 5
1. D
2. C
3. D
4. A
5. B

Comprehension of Expository Text

Activity 1
1. C
2. B
3. B
4. C
5. A
6. C
7. B
8. A

Activity 2
1. C
2. A
3. B
4. B
5. C
6. C
7. C
8. D
9. A

Activity 3
1. B
2. C
3. A
4. D
5. B
6. D
7. C
8. B

Comprehension of Recreational Selections
1. C
2. B
3. C
4. A
5. C
6. C
7. D
8. D
9. D
10. A

Comprehension of Functional Text
1. B
2. C
3. A
4. C
5. A
6. D
7. A

Cause and Effect
1. C
2. C
3. D
4. B
5. B
6. B
7. B
8. C
9. C
10. C
11. B
12. C
13. A

Reading Vocabulary
1. B
2. A
3. C
4. C
5. A
6. B
7. B
8. C
9. A
10. B

Capitalization
1. A   9. B
2. A   10. B
3. B   11. A
4. C   12. C
5. C
6. B
7. B
8. A

Punctuation
1. A
2. B
3. B
4. A
5. B
6. B
7. C
8. C
9. B
10. D

Usage
1. B
2. A
3. C
4. A
5. C
6. A
7. C
8. D
9. B
10. C

Sentence Structure
1. C
2. C
3. C
4. D
5. C
6. D
7. C

Study Skills
1. C
2. D
3. C
4. A
5. C
6. B
7. B
8. A
9. B
10. A
11. A
12. B
13. A
14. B
15. C

Study Skills, Cont'd.
16. A
17. D
18. C
19. A
20. B
21. A

Contractions
1. a. you're we're
   b. she's there's
 . c. he'll can't
 . d. you'll they're
2. a. can't
   b. doesn't
   c. Won't
   d. Isn't
3. a. we couldn't
   b. I shouldn't
   c. they wouldn't
   d. you wouldn't
   e. he wouldn't
   f. I'd
   g. she wouldn't
   h. she'd
4. a. Isn't
   b. They're
   c. It's there's
   d. can't, it's
   e. Where's

Activity 2
1. D
2. B
3. A
4. B
5. A
6. C
7. C

Spelling
Activity 1
1. bear
2. fox
3. lion
4. koala
5. tiger
6. elephant
7. alligator
8. snake
9. ostrich
10. giraffe

Spelling Activity 2
1. famous
   fast
   file
   first
2. man
   manners
   many
   map
3. brain
   brick
   brother
   brought
4. cracker
   critter
   crow
   crust

Spelling Activity 3
1. tame
2. eat
3. team
4. now
5. ton

Spelling Activity 4
1. dishes
2. trays
3. boxes
4. watches
5. socks
6. plates
7. words
8. parties
9. horses
10. taxis
11. puppies
12. boys
13. movies
14. lunches
15. candies
16. berries

Spelling

Activity 5
1. B
2. D
3. B
4. A
5. D
6. C
7. A
8. D
9. A
10. B
11. C
12. A
13. A
14. C
15. D
16. A
17. B
18. A
19. A
20. D
21. C
22. D

Activity 6
1. A
2. C
3. C
4. B
5. C
6. D

Activity 7
1. A
2. B
3. A
4. D
5. A
6. C

Activity 8
1. A
2. C
3. B
4. C
5. A
6. D
7. D
8. D
9. B
10. C
11. C
12. B
13. D

Capitalization

Activity 1
1. A
2. C
3. C
4. A
5. C
6. C
7. D

Activity 2
1. A
2. D
3. D
4. C
5. B
6. B
7. A
8. D

Synonyms
1. B
2. C
3. C
4. A
5. D
6. B
7. A
8. B

9. A
10. C
11. B
12. D

Antonyms
1. C
2. B
3. A
4. D
5. B
6. B
7. A
8. A
9. B
10. A
11. D
12. C

Word Analysis

Activity 1
1. D
2. D
3. B
4. C
5. A

Activity 2
1. A
2. B
3. B
4. C
5. A
6. D
7. B

Activity 3
1. C
2. A
3. B
4. B
5. D
6. A

NOTES

MATH

Practice Skill: ADDITION

Expectation: Solve problems using addition.

Tip: When you recopy addition problems, be sure to line up the digits so that all the digits in the ones place are directly beneath each other, the tens are directly beneath all the other tens, and the hundreds are in the hundreds column.

Solve the following problem and choose the correct answer.

1. 6 + 3 =

   o a. 10
   o b. 7
   o c. 3
   o d. 9

2. 4 + 6 =

   o a. 10
   o b. 6
   o c. 8
   o d. 12

3. 5 + 6 =

   o a. 12
   o b. 10
   o c. 11
   o d. 9

4. 27 + 32 =

   o a. 69
   o b. 59
   o c. 55
   o d. 95

5.   8 + 4 =

   o a. 10
   o b. 12
   o c. 16
   o d. 4

6.   33 + 23 + 10 =

   o a. 76
   o b. 56
   o c. 57
   o d. 66

7.   267 + 344 =

   o a. 611
   o b. 511
   o c. 601
   o d. 501

8.   7 + 3 + 5 =

   o a. 15
   o b. 16
   o c. 10
   o d. 14

9.   6042 + 3021 =

   o a. 9163
   o b. 9063
   o c. 7046
   o d. 9073

10.   51 + 10 =

   o a. 510
   o b. 65
   o c. 52
   o d. 61

11.   80 + 40 =

    o a. 120
    o b. 1200
    o c. 100
    o d. 130

12.   36 + 6 =

    o a. 39
    o b. 42
    o c. 32
    o d. 44

13.   6 + 44 =

    o a. 104
    o b. 50
    o c. 68
    o d. 72

14.   37 + 12 =

    o a. 59
    o b. 58
    o c. 49
    o d. 54

15.   130 + 27 =

    o a. 49
    o b. 327
    o c. 357
    o d. 157

16.   19 + 17 + 16=

    o a. 52
    o b. 32
    o c. 42
    o d. 53

Practice Skill: SUBTRACTION

Expectation: Solve problems using subtraction.

Tip: When you recopy these problems, be sure to line up the numbers correctly. It is important to subtract ones from ones, tens from tens, and hundreds from hundreds.

Solve each problem and choose the correct answer.

1. $19 - 17 =$

    o a. 2
    o b. 12
    o c. 36
    o d. 6

2. $17 - 9 =$

    o a. 26
    o b. 8
    o c. 9
    o d. 12

3. $74 - 9 =$

    o a. 65
    o b. 83
    o c. 75
    o d. 45

4. $60 - 6 =$

    o a. 66
    o b. 56
    o c. 54
    o d. 64

5. 774 − 22 =

    o a. 652
    o b. 752
    o c. 796
    o d. none of the above

6. 96 − 17 =

    o a. 69
    o b. 88
    o c. 59
    o d. none of the above

7. 27 − 9 =

    o a. 18
    o b. 27
    o c. 16
    o d. none of the above

8. 734 − 9 =

    o a. 624
    o b. 724
    o c. 725
    o d. none of the above

9. 73 − 8 =

    o a. 15
    o b. 81
    o c. 66
    o d. none of the above

10. 89 − 55 =

    o a. 34
    o b. 44
    o c. 54
    o d. 24

11.   17 – 8

    o a. 8
    o b. 9
    o c. 11
    o d. none of the above

12.   68 – 3 =

    o a. 55
    o b. 71
    o c. 65
    o d. none of the above

13.   383 – 83 =

    o a. 200
    o b. 300
    o c. 306
    o d. none of the above

14.   100 –97 =

    o a. 7
    o b. 17
    o c. 3
    o d. none of the above

15.   127 – 27 =
    o a. 227
    o b. 200
    o c. 100
    o d. none of the above

16.   237 – 137 =

    o a. 137
    o b. 100
    o c. 160
    o d. none of the above

Practice Skill: MULTIPLICATION

Expectation: Solve multiplication problems involving groups of
2s, 5s, and 10s.

Tip: Use drawings to illustrate how many groups are being multiplied how many times. Remember that multiplication is repeated addition.

Solve each problem and choose the correct answer.

1. $2 \times 3 =$

   o a. 2
   o b. 5
   o c. 6
   o d. 3

2. $5 \times 5 =$

   o a. 5
   o b. 10
   o c. 15
   o d. 25

3. $10 \times 6 =$

   o a. 60
   o b. 16
   o c. 70
   o d. 120

4. $4 \times 5 =$

   o a. 4
   o b. 9
   o c. 45
   o d. 20

5.   2 x 6 =

  o a. 2
  o b. 8
  o c. 12
  o d. 18

6.   5 x 7 =

  o a. 12
  o b. 25
  o c. 35
  o d. 30

7.   10 x 7 =

  o a. 17
  o b. 170
  o c. 107
  o d. 70

8.   10 x 10 =

  o a. 10
  o b. 20
  o c. 110
  o d. 100

9.   5 x 1 =

  o a. 5
  o b. 50
  o c. 6
  o d. 51

10.   9 x 2 =

  o a. 9
  o b. 92
  o c. 18
  o d. 11

Practice Skill: DIVISION

Expectation: Students will solve simple division problems.

Tip: Use drawings to illustrate how many items can be divided into how many groups.

Solve each problem and choose the correct answer.

1.　$15 \div 1 =$

　　o　a. 1
　　o　b. 10
　　o　c. 15
　　o　d. 0

2.　$15 \div 3 =$

　　o　a. 3
　　o　b. 15
　　o　c. 5
　　o　d. 18

3.　$10 \div 2 =$

　　o　a. 2
　　o　b. 5
　　o　c. 8
　　o　d. 20

4.　$20 \div 4 =$

　　o　a. 5
　　o　b. 10
　　o　c. 15
　　o　d. 4

5. $10 \div 5 =$

    o a. 5
    o b. 10
    o c. 15
    o c. 2

6. $24 \div 3 =$

    o a. 7
    o b. 8
    o c. 27
    o d. 12

7. $24 \div 8 =$

    o a. 3
    o b. 7
    o c. 32
    o d. 12

8. $12 \div 2 =$

    o a. 2
    o b. 12
    o c. 14
    o d. 6

9. $12 \div 3 =$

    o a. 2
    o b. 12
    o c. 4
    o d. 6

10. $12 \div 4 =$

    o a. 2
    o b. 12
    o c. 6
    o d. 3

Practice Skill: PROBLEM SOLVING – Number Sense and
                Numeration

Expectations: Identify numbers to 1000 and place value of digits
to the thousands place. Recognize expanded forms of numbers.
Skip count by 2s, 5s, and 10s. Order and compare whole numbers
and fractions by using the symbols < , > , and = .

Tip: Use a number line or drawings to help check your answers to
these exercises.

**ACTIVITY # 1 -- Look at the number and directions in bold type. Then
choose the correct answer.**

1.   564   Choose the numeral that is in the hundreds place.

        o a. 4
        o b. 5
        o c. 6
        o d. 500

2.   634   Choose the numeral that is in the tens place.

        o a. 3
        o b. 4
        o c. 6
        o d. 30

3.   425   Choose the numeral that is in the ones place.

        o a. 4
        o b. 2
        o c. 5
        o d. 1

4.   729   Choose the numeral that is in the hundreds place.

    o a. 7
    o b. 2
    o c. 9
    o d. 20

5.   501   Choose the numeral in the tens place.

    o a. 5
    o b. 0
    o c. 1
    o d. 01

ACTIVITY # 2 -- Choose the correct answer.

1.   5 tens 6 ones =

    o a. 56
    o b. 506
    o c. 65
    o d. 561

2.   3 hundreds 4 tens 5 ones =

    o a. 300405
    o b. 30045
    o c. 3045
    o d. 345

3.   752 =

    o a. 70 + 5 + 2
    o b. 70 + 50+2
    o c. 700 + 50 + 2
    o d. 7 + 5 + 2

4. Which is an even number?

    o   a.   10
    o   b.   3
    o   c.   7
    o   d.   19

5. Which numeral stands for fifteenth?

    o   a.   5
    o   b.   51
    o   c.   50
    o   d.   15

6. Which statement is true?

    o   a. $6 > 2$
    o   b. $6 < 2$
    o   c. $6 = 2$
    o   d. $2 > 6$

7. 2 , 4 , ___ , 8 , 10 , 12   Which number belongs in the blank?

    o   a.   2
    o   b.   5
    o   c.   6
    o   d.   7

8. 5 , 10 , 15 , ___, 25 , 30   Which number belongs in the blank?

    o   a.   15
    o   b.   20
    o   c.   16
    o   d.   21

9. Which number has a 6 in the hundreds place?

    o   a.   5063
    o   b.   5603
    o   c.   3056
    o   d.   6035

10. Which number has a 4 in the tens place?

    o a. 1234
    o b. 4321
    o c. 3412
    o d. 3142

11. Which is the <u>odd</u> number?

    o a. 14
    o b. 13
    o c. 22
    o d. 60

12. Which statement is true?

    o a. $\frac{5}{4} < 1$

    o b. $\frac{3}{4} = 1$

    o c. $\frac{4}{4} = 1$

    o d. $\frac{3}{4} > 1$

13. Six people share a pizza. Each person gets an equal part. Which parts does each person get?

    o a. $\frac{1}{2}$

    o b. $\frac{1}{4}$

    o c. 6

    o d. $\frac{1}{6}$

Practice Skills: Geometry and Spatial Sense

Expectation: Describe and classify geometric shapes according to the number and shape of faces, edges and vertices. (Circle, triangle, square, rectangle, sphere, pyramid, cube, rectangular prism.) Identify symmetrical shapes.

Tip: To help you understand the concepts of geometry, put shapes together and take them apart to form other shapes.

Choose the best answer.

1. Which circle shows an example of symmetry?

o a.   o b. 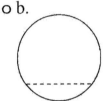   o c.   o d.

2. What shapes are in this picture?

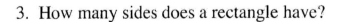

    o a. two triangles and 1 square
    o b. 2 squares and 1 triangle
    o c. 1 rectangle, 2 squares, and a triangle
    o d. 3 rectangles and 1 triangle

3. How many sides does a rectangle have?

    o a. 3
    o b. 2
    o c. 5
    o d. 4

4. How many sides does a cube have?

    o a. 6
    o b. 4
    o c. 2
    o d. 5

5. Which objects show examples of symmetry?

o a.   o b.   o c.   o d.

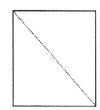   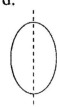

6. Which figure contains 2 triangles?

oa.   ob.   oc.   od.

 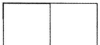  

7. Which item contains a pair of ellipses or ovals?

o a.   o b.   o c.   o d.

 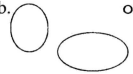 

8. Which figure is a cylinder?

o a.   o b.   o c.   o d.

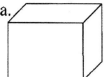  

9. Which figure is a rectangular prism?

o a.   o b.   o c. 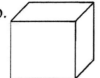   o d.

10. _____ figures are exactly the same size and shape.

    o a. Congruent
    o b. Similar
    o c. Geometric
    o d. Fraction

11. _____ triangles have the same shape but not the same size.

    o a. Congruent
    o b. Similar
    o c. Geometric
    o d. Fraction

12. How many corners does this figure have?

    o a. three
    o b. four
    o c. five
    o d. six

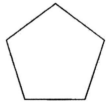

13. How many faces does this figure have?

    o a. three
    o b. four
    o c. five
    o d. six

14. Which coordinate gives the location of the star?

o a. B 3
o b. A 2
o c. C 3
o d. D 2

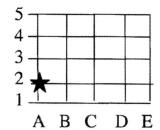

15. Which coordinate gives the location of the star?

o a. C 3
o b. B 2
o c. D 1
o d. A 3

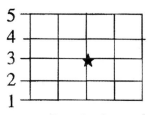

16. Which coordinate gives the location of the star?

o a. E 1
o b. D 4
o c. A 1
o d. E 4

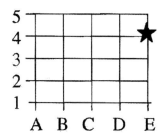

Practice Skill: PROBLEM SOLVING – Measurement

Expectations: Use various units of measure, including inches or centimeters. Tell time to the nearest five minutes. Determine the duration of time intervals in hours.

Tip: Practice counting by 5s to help you tell time on an analog clock.

Answer the following questions.

1. How long is the pencil?

 o a. 2 inches
 o b. 4 inches
 o c. 4 centimeters
 o d. 5 meters

2. How long is the eraser?

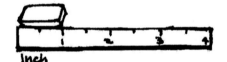

 o a. 1 inch
 o b. 2 inches
 o c. 1 centimeter
 o d. ½ inch

3. Which clock says 3:20?

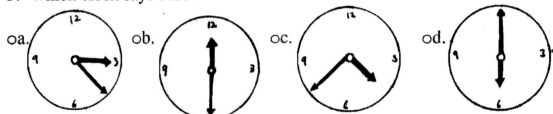

4. Which clock says 4:55?

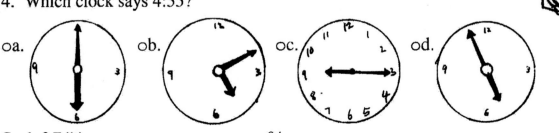

5. Which clock says 9:15?

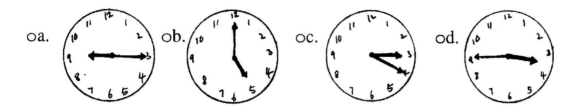

oa.　ob.　oc.　od.

6. How many hours pass between 9:00AM and 5:00PM?

   o a. 6 hours
   o b. 4 hours
   o c. 14 hours
   o d. 8 hours

7. How many hours pass between 8:00PM and 6:00AM?

   o a. 14 hours
   o b. 2 hours
   o c. 10 hours
   o d. 8 hours

8. How many hours pass between 8:00 a.m. and 8:00 p.m.?

   o a. 10 hours
   o b. 12 hours
   o c. 24 hours
   o d. 8 hours

9. Which sentence is true?

   o a. 1 foot > 1 yard
   o b. 1 foot = 36 inches
   o c. 1 foot = 12 inches
   o d. 1 foot < 1 inch

10. Which sentence is true?

    o a. 1 minute = 24 seconds
    o b. 1 hour = 60 minutes
    o c. 1 day > 14 hours
    o d. 32° is below 0 on a thermometer

11. What would be the best English unit to measure the length of a worm?

    o a. inch
    o b. centimeter
    o c. pound
    o d. ounce

12. What would be the best metric unit of measure to weigh a piece of tissue?

    o a. centimeter
    o b. pound
    o c. kilogram
    o d. gram

13. Which metric unit would you use to measure the distance from Los Angeles to New York?

    o a. kilogram
    o b. kilometer
    o c. mile
    o d. gram

14. Which metric unit would you use to measure the weight of an elephant?

    o a. kilogram
    o b. kilometer
    o c. meter
    o d. ton

15. How many centimeters long is the tip of the toothbrush that contains the bristles?

- o a. 11 cm
- o b. 10 cm
- o c. 1 ½ cm
- o d. 8 cm

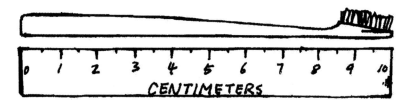

16. Mark the correct answer that matches the time on the clock.

- o a. 3:09
- o b. 6:45
- o c. 9:20
- o d. 4:45

17. According to the clock above, in 15 minutes it will be

- o a. 4:00.
- o b. 5:00.
- o c. 9:30.
- o d. 3:30.

The class photos at school start at 9:00 a.m. with the first grade. The second grade class photos begin one-half hour later. The third grade starts thirty minutes after the second grade.

18. What time will the second grade have their pictures taken?

- o a. 9:15
- o b. 9:30
- o c. 9:45
- o d. 10:00

19. If the pattern continues and the classes stay on time, what time will the fourth grade have their photos taken?

- o a. 9:30
- o b. 10:00
- o c. 10:30
- o d. 11:00

MAY

Sun	Mon	Tues	Wed	Thurs	Fri	Sat
1	2	3	4	5	6	7
8	9	10	11	12	13	14
15	16	17	18	19	20	21
22	23	24	25	26	27	28
29	30	31				

20. How many Saturdays are there in the above calendar of May?

- o a. 8
- o b. 4
- o c. 5
- o d. 1

21. What is the date of the third Wednesday?

- o a. 4
- o b. 30
- o c. 18
- o d. 19

22. What day is the 16th of May?

- o a. Monday
- o b. Tuesday
- o c. Wednesday
- o d. Friday

23. On what day of the week is June 1?

- o a. Sunday
- o b. Tuesday
- o c. Wednesday
- o d. Thursday

Practice Skill: PROBLEM SOLVING –
 Patterns and Relationships

Expectation: Solve problems involving number patterns.

Tip: Look for the differences between each number in the
pattern. Do you add or subtract as you move from one number to
the next within the pattern?

**Look at each number pattern. Choose the answer that completes the
pattern.**

1. 232, ___ , 234, 235

   o a. 234
   o b. 231
   o c. 243
   o d. 233

2. 330, 340, ___ , 360, 370

   o a. 350
   o b. 370
   o c. 341
   o d. 345

3. 1, 4, 7, ___ , 13, 16

   o a. 12
   o b. 10
   o c. 15
   o d. 12

4. ___ , 30, 35, 40, 45

   o a. 10
   o b. 20
   o c. 25
   o d. 29

5. 60, 50, 40, ___ , 20, 10

   o a. 70
   o b. 50
   o c. 30
   o d. 0

Practice Skill: PROBLEM SOLVING – Fractions

Expectation: Understand that fractions can refer to parts of a set and parts of a whole. Recognize common fractions, compare unit fractions up to 1/12, and recognize fractions of a whole and parts of a group. (e.g., ¼ of a pie, 2/3 of 15 balls)

Tip: When you are working out problems involving fractions, it often helps to draw diagrams. For example, when you want to solve 2/3 of 6, draw six lines, divide them into 3 equal groups (thirds), and add the number of lines within 2 of the 3 parts. When you are at home, use toothpicks or scraps of paper that you can separate into groups.

Choose the best answer to each of the following questions.

1. What fraction names the shaded part of the shape?

  o a. $\dfrac{1}{5}$

  o b. $\dfrac{1}{12}$

  o c. $\dfrac{2}{6}$

  o d. $\dfrac{2}{12}$

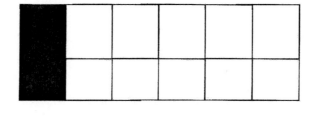

2. What fraction describes the shaded circles?

  o a. $\dfrac{3}{3}$

  o b. $\dfrac{1}{3}$

  o c. $\dfrac{2}{3}$

  o d. $\dfrac{3}{4}$

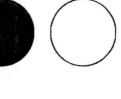

3. Which figure is 1/3 shaded?

 oa.   ob.   oc.   od.

4. What part is shaded?

    o a. $\frac{2}{4}$ o b. $\frac{1}{3}$ o c. $\frac{2}{5}$ o d. $\frac{2}{3}$

ACTIVITY # 2

1. What part is <u>not</u> shaded?

   o a. $\frac{1}{4}$ o b. $\frac{1}{3}$ o c. $\frac{1}{2}$ o d. $\frac{2}{3}$

2. What part is <u>not</u> shaded?

o a. $\frac{2}{4}$ o b. $\frac{1}{3}$ o c. $\frac{3}{4}$ o d. $\frac{1}{4}$

3. What part is shaded?

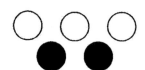

o a. $\frac{2}{4}$ o b. $\frac{1}{3}$ o c. $\frac{2}{5}$ o d. $\frac{2}{3}$

4. What part is <u>not</u> shaded?

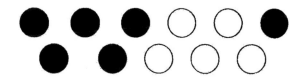

o a. $\frac{5}{11}$ o b. $\frac{1}{3}$ o c. $\frac{1}{5}$ o d. $\frac{5}{6}$

5. . What part is shaded?

   ○ a. $\frac{4}{3}$　　○ b. $\frac{2}{5}$　　　○ c. $\frac{1}{2}$ or $\frac{4}{8}$　　○ d. $\frac{1}{4}$

6. What part is not shaded?

   ○ a. $\frac{2}{3}$　　○ b. $\frac{2}{6}$ or $\frac{1}{3}$　　○ c. $\frac{3}{5}$　　　○ d. $\frac{4}{8}$ or $\frac{1}{2}$

7. Which pattern shows the fractions from largest to the smallest part of a whole?

   ○ a.　$\frac{1}{8}$　$\frac{1}{12}$　$\frac{1}{4}$　$\frac{1}{2}$

   ○ b.　$\frac{1}{12}$　$\frac{1}{10}$　$\frac{1}{8}$　$\frac{1}{4}$

   ○ c.　$\frac{1}{2}$　$\frac{1}{3}$　$\frac{1}{4}$　$\frac{1}{5}$　$\frac{1}{6}$

   ○ d.　$\frac{1}{5}$　$\frac{2}{5}$　$\frac{3}{5}$　$\frac{4}{5}$

8. Sharon and Mark cut a cookie into 6 equal pieces. Mark ate 3 of the pieces. What part of the cookie was left?

   ○ a. $\frac{3}{3}$　　○ b. $\frac{6}{6}$　　　○ c. $\frac{3}{6}$ or $\frac{1}{2}$　　○ d. $\frac{6}{3}$

Shawna poured lemonade for some thirsty friends. Tara asked for one-half of a glass of lemonade. Joel asked for one-fourth of a glass. Marquis wanted less than Joel.

9. Who asked for the most lemonade?

   ○ a. Shawna
   ○ b. Tara
   ○ c. Joel
   ○ d. Marquis

10. Whose glass was 1/8 full?

   ○a. Shawna　　○c. Joel
   ○b. Tara　　　○d. Marquis

Practice Skill: PROBLEM SOLVING –
            Data Analysis, Statistics, and Probability

Expectation: Solve problems using information from graphs.

Tip: When reading graphs, start by looking for titles and labels. If you read across the top or bottom of the chart, what do you see? If you read down the sides of the chart, what do you learn? To locate exact information, touch the graph lines with your fingers and follow them. This will help you avoid careless mistakes.

Exercise # 1 -- Use the chart to answer the following questions.

Favorite Food	Child							Adult						
	1	2	3	4	5	6	7	1	2	3	4	5	6	7
Pizza														
Ice Cream														
Salad														
Taco														
Rice														

1. How many adults like pizza the best?

   o a. 3
   o b. 7
   o c. 2
   o d. 1

2. How many more children than adults like ice cream?

   o a. 7
   o b. 2
   o c. 5
   o d. 3

3. How many people like salad the best?

    o a. 7
    o b. 8
    o c. 9
    o d. 10

4. How many children were part of the survey?

    o a. 30
    o b. 14
    o c. 7
    o d. 12

5. What was the most popular food among children?

    o a. pizza
    o b. ice cream
    o c. salad
    o d. tacos

6. How many people were part of the survey all together?

    o a. 13
    o b. 15
    o c. 28
    o d. 29

Review --Exercise # 2

1. Counting by ones, what number comes after 59?

    o a. 58
    o b. 69
    o c. 60
    o d. 97

2. How many hundreds are in 658?

    o a. 8
    o b. 5
    o c. 4
    o d. 6

3. How many of these numbers are less than 447?   778   459   439   447

    o a. 2
    o b. 3
    o c. 1
    o d. 4

4. What symbol correctly completes the number sentence below?

$$16 \boxed{} 8 = 8$$

    o a. +
    o b. −
    o c. x
    o d. ÷

5. If you are the fifth person in line, which person is in front of you?

    o a. fourth
    o b. sixth
    o c. second
    o d. seventh

6. What will make the number sentences true?

    _____ + 5 = 13   13 - _____ = 5

    o a. 2
    o b. 18
    o c. 7
    o d. 8

7. There are 20 students in a class. Each one brought in 3 pictures for a class collage. What is the fastest way to calculate the number of pictures they brought in all together?

    o a. divide
    o b. subtract
    o c. multiply
    o d. add

8. If you put these numbers in order from smallest to largest, which would be the first?   1000   702   720   719

   o a. 1000
   o b. 702
   o c. 720
   o d. 719

9. Which number fits the blank to make it correct? $17 + 5 + 3 = $ _____

   o a. 7
   o b. 15
   o c. 25
   o d. 27

10. Using the numbers in the circles, what is the largest number that can be made?

   o a. 236
   o b. 623
   o c. 632
   o d. 326

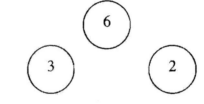

11. Using the numbers in the circles, what is the smallest number that can be made with a 2 in the ones place?

   o a. 623
   o b. 236
   o c. 362
   o d. 326

12. Using each numeral only once, what is the largest number that can be made with a 5, 0, and 9?

   o a. 509
   o b. 905
   o c. 950
   o d. 590

12. What number is greater than 279 but less than 289?

   o a. 294   o b. 298
   o c. 282   o d. 278

Practice Skill: PROBLEM SOLVING – Procedures

Expectation: Read and solve simple mathematical situations.

> Tip: When trying to solve a word problem, read through the entire problem carefully. Look for key words when deciding which procedure to use to solve a problem. (Addition words – in all, altogether. Subtraction words – how many more, how many fewer, how many left.) After solving the problem, read the question again and double check to make sure that your answer makes sense with all the information given in the problem.

ACTIVITY # 1 - Read each problem and choose the number sentence that correctly solves the problem.

1. Michele has 28 cat stickers. She has 9 dog stickers. How many more cat stickers than dog stickers does she have?

   o a. $28 + 9 = 37$ more dog stickers
   o b. $28 + 9 = 37$ more cat stickers
   o c. $28 - 9 = 19$ more cat stickers
   o d. none of the above

2. Three classes sold tickets to the school play. They sold a total of 98 tickets. The students in Mr. Javier's class sold 33 tickets to the play. Mrs. Kim's class sold 27 tickets. How many more tickets did Mr. Javier's class sell than Mrs. Kim's class?

   o a. $33 + 27 = 60$ more tickets
   o b. $98 - 33 = 65$ fewer tickets
   o c. $98 - 27 = 71$ more tickets
   o d. $33 - 27 = 6$ more tickets

3. In the problem above, how many tickets did the third class sell?
   o a. $27 + 6 = 33$ tickets
   o b. $98 - 33 = 65$ tickets
   o c. $98 + 33 + 27 =$ tickets
   o d. none of the above

4. Jenny is 8 years old. Sasha is 5 years older than Jenny. Victor is 2 years younger than Sasha. How old is Sasha?

- o a. 8 ñ 5 = 3 years old
- o b. 8 + 5 + 2 = 15 years old
- o c. 8 + 5 = 13 years old
- o d. none of the above

5. There are 54 boys in the second grade at Coldwater School. There are 62 girls attending second grade there. How many children are there in Coldwaterís second grade?

- o a. 54 + 62 = 116 students
- o b. 14 ñ 8 = 6 books
- o c. 14 + 8 = 22 books
- o d. none of the above

6. How much money is shown here?

- o a. 85¢
- o b. 45¢
- o c. 94¢
- o d. none of the above

7. What is the total of the coins shown here?

- o a. 78¢
- o b. 64¢
- o c. 74¢
- o d. none of the above

8. SuKay has 2 quarters, 1 dime, and 1 nickel. How much money does she have?

- o a. 31¢
- o b. 61¢
- o c. 65¢
- o d. none of the above

9. Tyrone has 4 dimes, 4 nickels, and 4 pennies. How much money does he have?

   o a. 44¢
   o b. 84¢
   o c. 64¢
   o d. none of the above

10. Which of these statements is true?

   o a. 70¢ = 5 dimes and 2 nickels
   o b. 1 quarter = 1 dime and 2 nickels
   o c. 2 quarters = 1 half-dollar
   o d. none of the above

11. Tawney has 95¢. She spent a quarter on a pack of gum. How much money does she have left?

   o a. 70¢
   o b. 75¢
   o c. 50¢
   o d. none of the above

12. Kyra has the amount of money shown here. She wants to buy a pencil grip for 79¢. Which of the following statements is true?

   o a. Kyra needs more money to buy the pencil grip.
   o b. Kyra has exactly enough money to buy the pencil grip.
   o c. If she buys the pencil grip, she will still have 6¢ left.
   o d. none of the above

13. If Kyra wants to buy the pencil grip and a 10¢ eraser, which of the following statements is true?

   o a. Kyra needs more money to buy the pencil grip and the eraser.
   o b. Kyra has exactly enough money to buy both items.
   o c. If she buys both items, she will have 5¢ left.
   o d. none of the above

14. Chelsea has 3 quarters and 2 dimes. If she buys a banana for 53¢, which statement is true?

   o a. Chelsea does not have enough money.
   o b. Chelsea will have 83¢ left.
   o c. Chelsea can buy 2 bananas.
   o d. Chelsea will still have 42¢.

15. Zoe has a half-dollar and 1 quarter. She spends 65¢ on a card. Which statement is true?

   o a. Zoe has 30¢ left.
   o b. Zoe could buy the card if she only gave the clerk 1 coin.
   o c. Zoe has 10¢ left.
   o d. none of the above

16. Postage stamps cost 34¢ each. Jose goes to the post office with 3 quarters. How many stamps can he buy?

   o a. 0
   o b. 1
   o c. 2
   o d. 3

17. Miriam has 8 coins that equal 80¢. Some are quarters and some are nickels, but she has no dimes. What coins does Mirium have?

   o a. 8 dimes
   o b. 5 quarters and nickels
   o c. 3 quarters and 1 nickel
   o d. 2 quarters and 6 nickels

18. Jona has 11 coins that equal $1.00. He has no quarters, but has dimes and nickels. What coins does Jonah have?

   o a. 4 quarters and 1 dime
   o b. 10 dimes and 1 nickel
   o c. 10 nickels and 1 dime
   o d. 9 dimes and 2 nickels

Activity #2 Look at the clocks to solve the problems.

1. The clerk left 15 minutes ago. What time did he leave?

    o a. 2:15
    o b. 3:15
    o c. 2:00
    o d. none of the above

2. The store will close for lunch in one-half hour.
   What time will it close?

    o a. 12:00
    o b. 1:00
    o c. 11:00
    o d. none of the above

3. Grandpa has been awake for 45 minutes.
   What time did he wake up?

    o a. 9:45
    o b. 9:00
    o c. 8:45
    o d. none of the above

4. This clock shows closing time. After that, it takes the clerk
   15 minutes to count the money and lock up the store.
   What time does the clerk leave the store?

    o a. 5:15
    o b. 5:45
    o c. 6:45
    o d. none of the above

5. Itís time to take a ten-minute break. What time does break end?

    o a. 4:45
    o b. 4:35
    o c. 5:55
    o d. none of the above

Practice Skill: PROBLEM SOLVING – Data Analysis and Graphing

Expectation: Read graphs and analyze information.

> Tip: When you first look at a graph or chart, study the important information on the sides, top, and bottom.

Use the graph to answer the following questions.

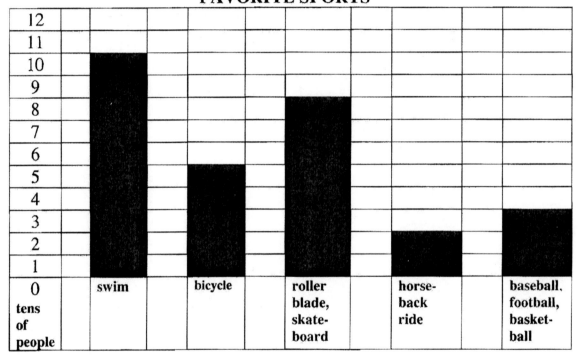

FAVORITE SPORTS

1. How many people like riding bicycles?

    o a. 5
    o b. 6
    o c. 50
    o d. 60

2. How many people like to fish?

    o a. 10
    o b. 100
    o c. 20
    o d. none of the above

3. What was the most popular sport?

  o a. swimming
  o b. bicycle riding
  o c. roller blading and skateboarding
  o d. none of the above

4. Which statement is true?

  o a. Horseback riding is one of the most popular sports.
  o b. Only 50 people were asked about their favorite sport.
  o c. More people said that they liked to ride bicycles more than ride horses.
  o d. Skateboarding is not considered a sport.

5. Eighty people said their favorite sport was

  o a. swimming.
  o b. bicycle riding.
  o c. roller blading and skateboarding.
  o d. none of the above

6. At least sixty people named _____ as their favorite sport.

  o a. bicycle riding
  o b. baseball, football, or basketball
  o c. horseback riding.
  o d. roller blading or skateboarding

7. Approximately how many people participated in the survey?

  o a. 50 people
  o b. 100
  o c. 200
  o d. 300

ADDITION

1. D
2. A
3. C
4. B
5. B
6. D
7. A
8. A
9. B
10. D
11. A
12. B
13. B
14. C
15. D
16. A

SUBTRACTION

1. A
2. B
3. A
4. C
5. B
6. D
7. A
8. C
9. D
10. A
11. B
12. C
13. B
14. C
15. C
16. B

MULTIPLICATION

1. C
2. D
3. A
4. D
5. C
6. C
7. D
8. D
9. A
10. C

DIVISION

1. C
2. C
3. B
4. A
5. D
6. B
7. A
8. D
9. C
10. D

PROBLEM SOLVING

Number Sense

Activity 1

1. B
2. A
3. C
4. A
5. B

Activity 2

1. A
2. D
3. C
4. A
5. D
6. A
7. C
8. B
9. B
10. D
11. B
12. C
13. D

Geometry

1. C
2. D
3. D
4. A
5. A, C, D
6. C
7. B

Geometry, Cont'd.

8. D
9. D
10. A
11. B
12. C
13. D
14. B
15. A
16. D

Measurement

1. C
2. A
3. A
4. D
5. A
6. D
7. C
8. B
9. C
10. B
11. A
12. D
13. B
14. A
15. C
16. D
17. B
18. B
19. C
20. B
21. C
22. A
23. C

Patterns

1. D
2. A
3. B
4. C
5. C

Fractions
1. D
2. D
3. D
4. A

Activity 2
1. B
2. D
3. C
4. A
5. C
6. D
7. C
8. C
9. B
10. D

Data Analysis
Exercise 1
1. C
2. B
3. D
4. B
5. B
6. D

Review – Exercise 2
1. C
2. D
3. C
4. B
5. A
6. D
7. C
8. B
9. C
10. C
11. C
12. C
13. B

Procedures
1. C
2. D
3. D
4. C
5. A
6. C

7. C
8. C
9. C
10. C
11. A
12. C
13. A
14. D
15. C
16. C
17. D
18. D

Activity 2
1. C
2. A
3. B
4. B
5. D

Data Analysis
1. C
2. D
3. A
4. C
5. C
6. D
7. D

HISTORY - SOCIAL SCIENCE

Practice Skill: MAP READING

Expectation: Use map skills to locate specific locations on a grid system. Understand essential map elements of title, scale, key, and direction.

> Tip: If you have trouble remembering directions, use this trick. Think about a clock face, but instead of the numbers at the quarter hour (12, 3, 6, and 9), substitute the letters N, E, S, and W. To remember which letter goes where, start at the top and say to yourself, "Never Eat Soggy Waffles!"

North America

North America is the third largest continent in the world. On North America the three largest countries in order of size are Canada, the United States, and Mexico. There are also 20 other small countries, which include many Caribbean islands.

Climates in North America range from always cold in the far north to always hot and wet in the far south, with milder climates in between. There are many mountains, plains, deserts, and bodies of water in North America. The Pacific Ocean and Atlantic Ocean border the west and east sides of North America.

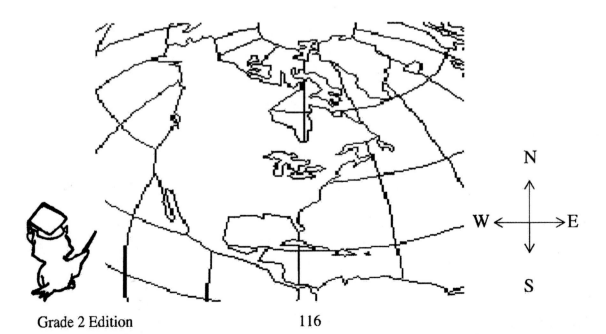

Choose the correct answer for each question.

1. The United States is a _____.

   o a. city
   o b. country
   o c. continent
   o d. river

2. _____ is the largest country in North America.

   o a. United States
   o b. Mexico
   o c. Canada
   o d. America

3. Which of the following rivers is not located in North America?

   o a. Amazon
   o b. Rio Grande
   o c. St. Lawrence
   o d. Mississippi

4. What is the highest mountain in North America?

   o a. Mt. Whitney
   o b. Mt. Everest
   o c. Mt. McKinley
   o d. Mt. Kilimanjaro

5. The ocean on the east side of North America is the

   _____.

   o a. Atlantic
   o b. Indian
   o c. Gulf of Mexico
   o d. Pacific

6. The _____ are surrounded by the United States and Canada.

   o a. Mississippi River and Missouri River
   o b. Sierra Nevada Mountains
   o c. Great Lakes
   o d. Appalachian Mountains

Latitude and Longitude

Many maps and globes have a grid line system that helps us locate exact locations. Latitude lines run horizontally, parallel to each other. Every latitude line is numbered by degrees. The equator, an imaginary line that divides the world into two sections (Northern Hemisphere and Southern Hemisphere), is located at zero degrees. The North Pole is at 90° north and the South Pole is at 90° south. The vertical lines on the map are called longitude lines. Zero degrees longitude is located in Greenwich, England. This line is called the Prime Meridian. The longitude lines are measured in degrees east and west.

Remember that these grid lines help us read maps and describe locations. They are not real lines that you can touch on the earth. If it is hard for you to remember which lines are which, try this trick: Think of the latitude lines as the rungs of a ladder that you can climb up or down, like "ladder-tude" lines.

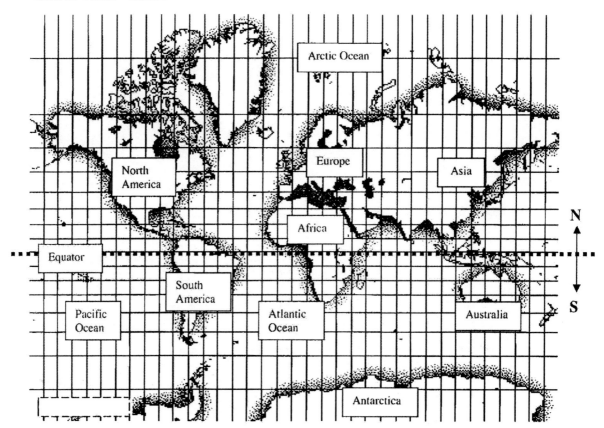

Read the question. Choose the best answer.

1. What is the largest continent south of the equator?

    o a. Europe
    o b. Australia
    o c. North America
    o d. Antarctica

2. What map grid line is at 0° latitude?

    o a. Prime Meridian
    o b. Equator
    o c. International date line
    o d. North Pole

3. What place is located at 90° south?

    o a. North Pole
    o b. Prima Meridian
    o c. United States
    o d. South Pole

4. What continents are located entirely in the northern hemisphere?

    o a. Arctic Circle, Europe, Africa
    o b. North America, South America, Asia
    o c. North America, Europe, Asia
    o d. South America, Africa, Australia, Antarctica

5. The Prime Meridian runs through the continents of

    o a. Europe, Africa, Antarctica
    o b. Australia, Africa, South America
    o c. Arctic Ocean, Atlantic Ocean
    o d. North America, South America, Antarctica

6. The fastest way to fly from the East Coast of the United States to the West Coast is to head in which direction?

    o a. north
    o b. south
    o c. east
    o d. west

Practice Skills: PEOPLE WHO HAVE MADE A DIFFERENCE IN OUR LIVES

Expectation: Be familiar with the lives of people from long ago and the recent past that have made a difference in our lives.

Tip: One way to become familiar with the lives and characters of people who have made important contributions to the world is to read biographies, the stories of their lives. A few of these interesting people are described in the exercises of this section.

Each exercise contains facts that describe a person who has made an important contribution to our country or to the world. Read the description and identify the person whose life is described.

1. He lived from 1706 – 1790 in the United States. He published *Poor Richard's Almanac,* founded the first lending library in America, invented bifocal glasses, and experimented with electricity. He signed the Declaration of Independence. He is

   o a. George Washington
   o b. Thomas Jefferson
   o c. Benjamin Franklin
   o d. Abraham Lincoln

2. He lived from 1732 – 1799. He led the army against the King of England in America's war for independence. He lived at Mount Vernon, his Virginia plantation, except for the time he served as the first President of the United States. He is

   o a. George Washington
   o b. Thomas Jefferson
   o c. Benjamin Franklin
   o d. Abraham Lincoln

3. He lived from 1742 – 1826. He wrote most of the Declaration of Independence. He designed his home at Monticello, Virginia. When he served as the third President of the United States, he bought land from France to make our country twice as large as it was. He is

  o a. George Washington
  o b. Thomas Jefferson
  o c. Benjamin Franklin
  o d. Abraham Lincoln

4. He was a great scientist and inventor who lived in Italy from 1564 – 1642. He was one of the first people to point a telescope at the stars. He was sent to jail for believing that the Earth moves around the Sun. He discovered that a swinging pendulum could help keep time. He is

  o a. Christopher Columbus
  o b. Marco Polo
  o c. Wolfgang Amadeus Mozart
  o d. Galileo Galilei

5. He was a scientist who lived in England from 1642 – 1727. He discovered the idea of gravity and three laws of motion. He invented a telescope that used mirrors to magnify. He is

  o a. King John
  o b. Sir Isaac Newton
  o c. Galileo Galilei
  o d. Edmond Halley

6. He lived in Austria from 1756 – 1791. He was a musical genius who began playing the harpsichord at age four. He composed his first pieces at the age of five. Before he was twenty years old, he had written 30 symphonies and two operas. His most famous operas are *The Magic Flute* and *The Marriage of Figaro*. He is

  o a. Sir Isaac Newton
  o b. Wolfgang Amadeus Mozart
  o c. Nicolas Copernicus
  o d. Marco Polo

7. She was a Shoshone Indian who lived from 1789 – 1812. In 1804, the famous explorers Lewis and Clark hired her to be their guide through the American wilderness. She traveled with her baby on that trip. She is

   o a. Abigail Adams
   o b. Martha Washington
   o c. Geronimo
   o d. Sacajawea

8. She lived from 1815 – 1913. She was a runaway slave who helped hundreds of other slaves escape north on the "Underground Railroad." During the Civil War she served as a nurse and a spy. She is

   o a. Sacajawea
   o b. Susan B. Anthony
   o c. Harriet Tubman
   o d. Abigail Adams

9. She lived in America from 1821 – 1910. In 1849 she was the first American woman to receive a medical degree. She later established a hospital for women and children, and a medical college for women. She is

   o a. Emily Dickinson
   o b. Susan B. Anthony
   o c. Eleanor Roosevelt
   o d. Elizabeth Blackwell

10. She lived in America from 1820 – 1906. She hated slavery. She worked for years to get women the right to vote and control property. She published a newspaper and started a women's rights organization. Her likeness appears on a U.S. silver dollar. She is

   o a. Elizabeth Blackwell
   o b. Harriet Tubman
   o c. Eleanor Roosevelt
   o d. Susan B. Anthony

11. They were two brothers born in Ohio in the late 1800s. They showed great mechanical talent in their bicycle repair shop. They built and flew their own gliders. In 1903 they attached a gasoline engine to one of their gliders and flew for 12 seconds. They were the first to achieve powered flight. They are

- o a. Lewis and Clark
- o b. Wilbur and Orville Wright
- o c. The Earp Brothers
- o d. Butch Cassidy and the Sundance Kid

12. She was born in Poland in 1867. Because at that time women were not allowed to study at the university in Poland, she moved to Paris to study. She graduated first in her class in physics and second in her class in math. She studied magnetism and radioactivity, and discovered the element radium. She won the Nobel Prize for Physics in 1903. She is

- o a. Isadora Duncan
- o b. Georgia O'Keefe
- o c. Helen Keller
- o d. Marie Curie

13. He was born in Scotland in 1847. He moved with his family to Canada in 1870. He helped deaf people learn how to speak. He invented a way for electricity to carry sound. He invented the telephone in 1876 and founded his own telephone company the next year. He is

- o a. Albert Einstein
- o b. Claude Monet
- o c. Alexander Graham Bell
- o d. Thomas Edison

14. He was born in Germany in 1879. He worked in Switzerland as an office clerk when he published his ideas about matter and energy in the universe. His theory was called the Theory of Relativity. He won the Nobel Prize for Physics in 1923. He moved to the United States when the Nazis made life for Jews in Europe impossible. He was

- o a. Albert Einstein
- o b. Pablo Picasso
- o c. Pierre Curie
- o d. Charles Richter

15. He lived from 1847 – 1933 in the United States. He found it difficult to learn in school, and his mother taught him at home. He loved science and had his own laboratory at home by the time he was 10 years old. He invented more than 1,000 things, including a telegraph that transferred messages to a printer, a motion picture projector, a phonograph, and the light bulb. He is

- o a. Albert Einstein
- o b. Thomas Edison
- o c. Alexander Graham Bell
- o d. Robert Louis Stevenson

16. She lived in the United States from 1880 – 1968. At the age of 19 months, an illness made her blind, deaf, and unable to talk. A teacher taught her to learn to speak by feeling the vibrations in her throat, to read and write in Braille, and to understand what others were saying by having them spell words into her hands. In spite of her tremendous challenges, she graduated from college with honors and became a world-famous lecturer and author. She spent the rest of her life helping other deaf and blind people. She is

- o a. Maria Montessori
- o b. Marie Curie
- o c. Eleanor Roosevelt
- o d. Helen Keller

Practice Skill: INSTITUTIONS AND PRACTICES OF
                 GOVERNMENT

Expectation: Know how laws are made and carried out.

Tip: Not all governments and countries are organized the same way. For example, instead of a president who is elected by voters to lead the government, some countries have a king or queen who inherits the right to make leadership decisions. Sometimes elected officials share the duties of governments with a king or queen.

In the United States, the ideas and rules that our government must live by are written in our Constitution. Under our Constitution, there are 3 main branches or sections of our country's government. The three branches share the power and duties of running our country for all Americans. The President and his staff make up the Executive Branch of our government. The Legislative Branch is made up of our Senators and members of Congress who we elect to the House of Representatives. It is this group of officials who make the laws in our country. The judges of our courts are part of the third branch of government, the Judicial Branch. The members of the Judicial Branch make sure that our laws follow the Constitution and that people abide by the laws.

Read the question and choose the best answer.

1. The President is part of the _____ of our government.

   - o a. head
   - o b. Legislative Branch
   - o c. Executive Branch
   - o d. Judicial Branch

2. The Senators and members of the House of Representatives are part of the

   - o a. Appointed Branch
   - o b. Legislative Branch
   - o c. Judicial Branch
   - o d. Executive Branch

3. The judges and courts are part of the _____ Branch.

   - o a. Senate
   - o b. Legislative
   - o c. Executive
   - o d. Judicial

4. The Constitution

   - o a. is the framework of laws and rules of our government.
   - o b. is the President's airplane.
   - o c. is the same for every government.
   - o d. calls for a king or queen to lead the people.

ANSWER KEY
HISTORY-SOCIAL SCIENCE

North America
1. B
2. C
3. A
4. C
5. A
6. C

Latitude & Longitude
1. D
2. B
3. D
4. C
5. A
6. D

People
1. C
2. A
3. B
4. D
5. B
6. B
7. D
8. C
9. D
10. D
11. B
12. D
13. C
14. A
15. B
16. D

Government
1. C
2. B
3. D
4. A

SCIENCE

Practice Skill: PHYSICAL SCIENCE

Expectation: Understand some of the principles underlying the motion of objects.

Tip: In the area of physical science, you will need to know and understand:

- The way to change how something moves is to give it a push or a pull. The size of the change is related to the strength, or the amount of "force," of the push or pull.
- Tools and machines can be used to push or pull (forces) to make things move.
- Objects near the Earth fall to the ground unless something holds them up.
- Magnets can be used to make some objects move without being touched.
- Sound is made by vibrating objects and can be described by its pitch and volume.

Gravity and Motion

In 1666, a young man named Isaac Newton had an important thought that changed the way people view the world. While sitting in his garden, Newton saw an apple fall from a tree to the ground. At that moment, he realized that things fall to the ground because a force from the center of the earth pulls them down toward the earth's core. This force is called gravity. Without the force of gravity acting upon us and pulling us down to earth, we would be floating in space all the time! It is gravity that causes things to fall to the ground unless something is holding them up and away from the ground.

Newton also set out to prove that the earth has a force of gravity that pulls on the moon and keeps it orbiting (circling) around the earth. But Newton didn't stop there. He also proved that the force of gravity keeps the planets orbiting around the sun.

Newton discovered 3 Laws of Motion that he proved with mathematics. The First Law states that any object that is standing still will not move until it is pushed or pulled. Once the object is moving, it will remain moving in a straight line without any additional force. This tendency of an object not to change is called inertia. Newton's Second and Third Laws of Motion explain more about force.

Although these ideas sound tricky, if you think about a horse pulling a heavy wagon, you can see Newton's Law in action. When the wagon is standing still, the horse must work very hard to get it moving. It uses force to overcome inertia. Then, once the wagon starts moving, the horse doesn't have to work quite so hard. This is Newton's Law.

Read the question. Choose the best answer.

1. Gravity is
    - o a. inside an apple.
    - o b. what helps us fly.
    - o c. a force that pulls objects toward the earth.
    - o d. none of the above

2. Who first had the idea of gravity?
    - o a. Isaac Newton
    - o b. Galileo
    - o c. an apple grower
    - o d. 20th century scientists

1. Without gravity
    - o a. we would orbit around the sun.
    - o b. we would float above the earth.
    - o c. we would all be pulled to the center of the earth.
    - o d. none of the above

2. The word orbit most often refers to
    - o a. the path around a planet
    - o b. a web
    - o c. a rocket's speed
    - o d. a shining star

3. Gravity
    - o a. has nothing to do with the orbit of the planets.
    - o b. has nothing to do with our moon's orbit.
    - o c. has nothing to do with the earth's orbit of the sun.
    - o d. none of the above

4. Inertia
    - o a. keeps things still if they are not already moving.
    - o b. is the path around a planet.
    - o c. is a fancy kind of wagon.
    - o d. none of the above

5. Newton's First Law of Motion
    - o a. explains gravity.
    - o b. does not talk about force.
    - o c. talks about forces that push or pull.
    - o d. none of the above

Practice Skill: LIFE SCIENCE

Expectation: Know the sequential stages of life cycles for different animals and plants.

Tip: Living things have predictable—and very different--life cycles.   This section will help you focus on some of these similarities and differences.
    Think of how butterflies, frogs, chickens, and kittens are born and grow. Consider the difference between the natural life of a hundred-year-old oak tree and a petunia that might grow in a garden.   Then consider all the ways that animals and plants interact with each other. Learn all the positive and negative ways they affect each other.

Plants and Animals Need Each Other

Most living things need food, water, sunlight, and oxygen to survive and grow. Some also need minerals to stay healthy. Over a very long period of time, if a living thing has a hard time getting something it needs to survive, it may adapt to its environment and find a way to survive. This adaptation has made it possible for certain plants to grow deep in the ocean where there is no sunlight. These plants have adapted to get their energy from minerals and nutrients in the ocean, rather than from the sunlight.

Although some forms of life have adapted to life without sunshine, no living thing has learned to live without food. Food is what gives all living things the energy to live, to grow, to get rid of waste, and to reproduce. In nature, plants are the only living things that can manufacture their own food. Think of plants as food factories. They make enough food to keep themselves alive and they store the rest in their stems, roots, seeds, or fruit. Then people and animals eat the plants to get energy. This is the food chain that connects all living things and keeps us alive.

Plants make their food through a process we call photosynthesis. Photosynthesis starts when light hits the plant's leaves. A green chemical (called chlorophyll) in the leaf works with the light to split the water in the plant into its basic parts. Carbon dioxide enters the leaf through holes called stomates. When the carbon dioxide, water parts, and light come together in the plant, there is a chemical reaction and the plant makes sugar. At the same time, the plant releases oxygen. Oxygen is what people need to breathe. This part of the plant's work is called respiration. Now you can see why photosynthesis and respiration in plants keep animals and humans alive. But don't forget that it is the carbon dioxide that people exhale or "breathe out" that is a necessary part of photosynthesis. Humans and animals inhale or "breathe in" oxygen, and they exhale carbon dioxide. Plants take in carbon dioxide and give off oxygen during photosynthesis. We need each other to survive!

Read the question. Choose the best answer.

1. Most living things need _____ to survive and grow.

  o a. vegetables or meat
  o b. plant stems and roots
  o c. food, water, light, and oxygen
  o d. carbon dioxide

2. A plant that gets its energy from the ocean instead of the sun is an example of _____.

  o a. photosynthesis
  o b. respiration
  o c. adaptation
  o d. extinction

3. All living things need _____.

  o a. adaptation
  o b. food
  o c. sugar
  o d. ocean water

4. The only living things that manufacture their own food are _____.

  o a. people
  o b. factories
  o c. plants
  o d. stomates

5. Plants make food through a process called _____.

  o a. chlorophyll
  o b. photosynthesis
  o c. adaptation
  o d. food chain

6. Photosynthesis and respiration produce _____ .

- o a. sugar and oxygen
- o b. carbon dioxide
- o c. water and light
- o d. roots, stems, and leaves

7. Leaves contain a green chemical called _____ .

- o a. chlorophyll
- o b. energy
- o c. photosynthesis
- o d. stomates

8. The word exhale means _____ .

- o a. breathe out
- o b. get energy
- o c. eat
- o d. breath in

9. People exhale _____ .

- o a. oxygen
- o b. energy
- o c. carbon dioxide
- o d. water

10. Plants need _____ from people for photosynthesis.

- o a. sunlight
- o b. energy
- o c. oxygen
- o d. carbon dioxide

11. People need _____ from plants in order to breathe.

- o a. sunlight
- o b. energy
- o c. oxygen
- o d. carbon dioxide

12. The _____ keeps us alive and connects all living things.

   o a. food chain
   o b. animals
   o c. people
   o d. ocean

13. The word inhale means

   o a. breathe out
   o b. get energy
   o c. eat
   o d. breath in

14. The process in which plants give off oxygen is called

   o a. inhalation
   o b. exhalation
   o c. respiration
   o d. photosynthesis

15. _____ starts the process of photosynthesis.

   o a. Sugar
   o b. Sunlight
   o c. Chlorophyll
   o d. Oxygen

16. The stomates are _____ in the leaves.

   o a. water
   o b. holes
   o c. worms
   o d. green chemicals

Life Cycles

All living plants and animals have a life cycle in which they are born, they mature, and they die. They must reproduce in order to keep their species (particular kind of plant or animal) going. Some life cycles are very short, like the fruit fly that goes from an egg to an adult in one week. But some life cycles last for thousands of years. The oldest living thing is a bristlecone pine tree that is more than 4,760 years old! You can see it in the Inyo National Forest near Bishop, California.

As most animals grow from birth to adulthood, they change as they mature, but their outward appearance does not change all that much. For example, when a foal is born, everyone can tell it is a horse. It is much the same with giraffes, ducks, and most of the animal world. But there are some living things that undergo enormous changes in their appearance during their life cycles. They completely change forms during their lives. This series of changes is called metamorphosis.

The Metamorphosis of a Butterfly

Butterflies go through a complete metamorphosis during their lives. They have four separate phases in their life cycle: egg, larva, pupa, and adult. First the female lays tiny eggs on a plant. After anywhere from one week to one month, each egg hatches into a small caterpillar, called a larva. During the larva stage, the caterpillar eats and eats. It molts or sheds its skin as it gets bigger and bigger over the next two weeks. As the caterpillar matures, it looks for a safe place to pupate (change into a pupa or chrysalis). The caterpillar prepares to become a chrysalis by hanging upside down and attaching itself to a plant. It attaches itself to the plant with threads of silk. As it stays in the pupa stage, huge changes are happening, because an adult butterfly moth is developing. When metamorphosis is complete, the chrysalis splits open and an adult butterfly crawls out. At first, its wings and body are very soft and wrinkled, but in less than an hour its body and wings are dry and hard enough for it to fly away.

The Metamorphosis of a Frog

Frogs go through their own kind of metamorphosis, too. In their metamorphosis, a tadpole hatches out of the egg after about ten days in the water. The tadpole lives in the water, breathes with gills, and has a tail. As soon as the tadpole hatches, it sticks itself to weeds or grass in the water. After about a week, it will swim around and eat algae. As the tadpole grows, back legs begin to appear, and lungs start to form. It is starting to prepare for its life on land. After six to nine weeks, the tadpole starts to absorb its tail and gills. Now the tadpole will eat plants and dead insects floating on the water. Within 10 to 12 weeks, the tadpole quickly develops front legs. After its front legs form, the tadpole does not eat. It absorbs its tail for food. After twelve weeks, a froglet with a tiny tail stub has developed. Its mouth widens, its tail nearly disappears, its legs grow, and its lungs are almost fully formed at this stage. It can eat small bugs. It now spends most of its time out of the water. Once the frog finishes growing and has lost its tail, it is considered an adult frog.

Plant Life Cycles

Of course, all plants have life cycles, too, but they can be different from plant to plant. A plant that grows, makes flowers, fruit and seed, and then dies all in one growing season is called an annual. Perennials are plants that come back year after year without replanting, usually from underground parts. Then there are biennials that produce green leaves in one year, flowers the next year, and then die. But how do they keep their species going? Most plants make seeds in order to continue the life cycle. The wind can blow light seeds in the air and onto the ground. Other seeds are sticky and attach themselves to animals. When a seed settles in the ground and get enough light and water, it starts to germinate, or develop into a young plant. A seedling starts to grow out of the seed. Roots also start to grow. If the plant is a flowering plant, seeds form inside the flowers after bees pollinate it. Then the cycle is ready to begin again.

Read the question. Choose the best answer.

1. Which of the following statements is <u>not</u> true?

    o a. The life cycle of plants and animals includes birth, growth and maturity, and death.
    o b. All life cycles of living things last the same amount of time.
    o c. Fruit flies have a short life span.
    o d. During the life cycle, animals and plants change in many ways.

2. Metamorphosis is

    o a. when a foal grows into a horse.
    o b. when a bear cub grows into a bear.
    o c. when a puppy grows into a dog.
    o d. when a tadpole grows into a frog.

3. The life cycle of a butterfly includes

    o a. egg, antennae, wings, and silk.
    o b. egg, baby, and chrysalis.
    o c. egg, caterpillar, tail, wings.
    o d. egg, larva, pupa, and adult butterfly.

4. Another word for larva is

    o a. egg.
    o b. caterpillar.
    o c. pupa.
    o d. butterfly.

5. During which stage does the butterfly develop?

    o a. egg
    o b. larva
    o c. pupa
    o d. adult

6. The life cycle of a frog includes

    o a. egg, tadpole, froglet, and frog.
    o b. tadpole, legs, lungs, and tail.
    o c. gills, lungs, tail, and jaws.
    o d. egg, swim, breathe, and jump.

Practice Skill: EARTH SCIENCE

Expectation: Know the materials and resources that make up Earth. Know why scientists study fossils.

Tip: Earth science is where you learn about the natural resources of our world –its rocks, minerals, water, plants, and soil. There are many different kinds of rocks and minerals on our planet. Our soil is made partly from weathered rock and partly from organic (animal or plant) material. Of course, not all soil is the same. Depending on the contents of the soil, it may or may not be easy for plants to grow in it. All the parts of the earth affect each other.

   We need the earth's resources for food, fuel, and building materials. One way we learn about earth science is by studying fossils. They provide us evidence about the plants and animals that lived on our earth before us.

Rocks and Minerals

It is interesting to think that even though rocks come in so many different shapes, colors, and textures, there are only three ways that they are made.

Igneous rocks are made from molten magma (liquid rock from the center of the earth). Sometimes the magma comes to the surface of the earth when volcanoes erupt, but most of the time the magma cools deep underground and becomes solid there. Lava and granite are examples of igneous rocks.

Sedimentary rocks are "deposited" rocks made from sediment. Rocks are constantly being weathered and broken down into grains that are carried by the wind, rain, or the ocean tides. As these grains are deposited, they settle together with the remains of animals and plants. They get buried deeper and deeper over time. They are pressed and squeezed and cemented by minerals, until they form sedimentary rock. Sandstone, shale, and limestone are examples of sedimentary rocks. Coal is made from the squashed remains of swamps and forests that existed millions of years ago.

Sometimes igneous and sedimentary rocks are present when a volcano erupts or when the earth shifts. Such intense heat or pressure changes the rocks so much that they become a new kind of rock, called metamorphic rock. Marble is a changed form of limestone. Slate is metamorphosed shale.

No matter which kind of rock you look at, you will see that it is made of tiny grains or crystals. These crystals are called minerals. Minerals are not living things. A mineral is a chemical that forms naturally in the earth. There are thousands of minerals, but only about 30 that we see over and over again. Minerals come in all colors, shapes, sizes, and textures. Some rocks contain just one mineral, while other rocks contain several. Quartz, topaz, and diamonds are all minerals.

Read the question and choose the best answer.

1. _____ cools to form hard igneous rocks.

    o a. Water
    o b. Mountain soil
    o c. Magma
    o d. Mineral

2. _____ rock is called magma.

    o a. Melted or liquid
    o b. Mineral
    o c. River
    o d. Weathered

3. _____ are examples of igneous rocks.

    o a. Shale and limestone
    o b. Gold, silver, and diamonds
    o c. Marble and slate
    o d. Lava and granite

4. Rocks that are _____ are called metamorphic.

    o a. lava
    o b. liquid
    o c. changed
    o d. hot

5. A good description of sediment is _____ .

    o a. volcanic lava
    o b. tiny grains of rock that are deposited by wind or water
    o c. pressure
    o d. none of the above

6. _____ are examples of sedimentary rocks.

    o a. Shale and limestone
    o b. Gold, silver, and diamonds
    o c. Marble and slate
    o d. Lava and granite

7. _____ is a sedimentary rock that we use for fuel and heat.

- o a. Marble
- o b. Slate
- o c. Coal
- o d. Quartz

6. A _____ is a chemical that forms naturally in the earth.

- o a. rock
- o b. liquid
- o c. soil
- o d. mineral

7. Examples of minerals are _____.

- o a. quartz, topaz, and diamonds
- o b. sediment, rocks, and water
- o c. sandstone, shale, and limestone
- o d. magma, lava, and granite

8. Minerals are also called _____.

- o a. igneous
- o b. chemicals
- o c. crystals
- o d. rocks

11. Which of the following sentence is not true?

- o a. There are thousands of minerals in the earth.
- o b. Minerals come in all different sizes, textures, and colors.
- o c. Very few rocks contain minerals.
- o d. Minerals are not living things.

Fossils

Fossils are the remains or evidence of animals and plants that have been preserved naturally in rock. Any creature can become a fossil, as long as it is buried quickly. Most of the time, fossils are formed from the hard parts of animals and plants, such as shells, bones, teeth, or wood. Sometimes, though, the soft tissue reacts with minerals to form a cast or mold of the animal or plant. The process of changing from a living thing to a fossil takes millions of years.

Not all rocks contain fossils. Igneous and metamorphic rocks do not contain fossils because no living thing could withstand that kind of heat, pressure, or movement. Paleontologists (scientists who study fossils) know to look for fossils in different kinds of sedimentary rocks. Most fossils were formed in the ocean where sand and mud were deposited again and again to bury the animal or plant. That is why the fossils that are found most often are small animals with shells. But paleontologists have discovered some magnificent fossils of living things that were caught and buried in tar or ice. The La Brea Tar Pits in Los Angeles contain many fossils of saber-toothed cats and mammoths. In Siberia in northern Asia, paleontologists have discovered mammoths in the permafrost (permanently frozen ground). These mammoths have been extinct for more than 12,000 years!

Why are fossils important? They help us learn the history of the life on Earth, as well as the history of Earth, itself. Fossils tell us what extinct animals looked like and what their habits were. Trace fossils show the traces of footprints and the trails of animals that lived millions of years ago. Certain fossils, called index fossils are quite useful to geologists, the scientists who study rocks. Index fossils are from plants and animals that lived in many places, but not for a very long period of time. Those fossils help geologists know the age of different rocks and which rocks around the world were formed at the same time. Also, scientists on opposite sides of the ocean have found identical fossils of plants and animals that could not get across water. This tells us that long ago, these lands were joined at one time and there was no ocean between them. When paleontologists find shark's teeth in the desert, they know that at one time, ocean covered the area.

Read the question. Choose the best answer.

1. Fossils are the remains of _____ that have been naturally preserved in rock.

   - o a. minerals
   - o b. nonliving things
   - o c. plants and animals
   - o d. soil and sand

2. Fossils are found mainly in _____.

   - o a. marble
   - o b. sedimentary rock
   - o c. granite
   - o d. volcanoes

3. A paleontologist is _____.

   - o a. a scientist who studies fossils
   - o b. not a scientist, but a painter
   - o c. a scientist who studies rock formations
   - o d. a scientist who studies oceans

4. A geologist is _____.

   - o a. a person who makes jewelry
   - o b. a scientist who studies animals
   - o c. a scientist who studies rock formations
   - o d. a scientist who studies oceans

5. Which is <u>not</u> a reason that scientists study fossils?

   - o a. Fossils make them very rich.
   - o b. Fossils tell them about the development and habits of animals.
   - o c. Fossils prove the age of some rocks.
   - o d. Fossils tell them how Earth has changed over the years.

6. Trace fossils

   - o a. are the oldest fossils.
   - o b. are the newest fossils.
   - o c. help geologists know the age of certain rocks.
   - o d. show the travels and footprints of animals.

Practice Skills: INVESTIGATION AND EXPERIMENTATION

Expectation: Know the tools and terms used to conduct experiments and scientific investigation.

> Tip: The foundation of scientific investigation is careful observation and asking questions. A scientist will then formulate a hypothesis, or tentative answer to the question. Then she will think of a way to test her hypothesis by conducting an experiment and predicting the result. If the hypothesis is true, then she can expect a certain result. Finally, the scientist performs the experiment. She analyzes the data to see if the predicted results were achieved. If so, the results support the hypothesis. Sometimes the scientist modifies the hypothesis and starts all over again. This is not a failure. This is an important part of the scientific process and investigation.
>
> In second grade, you will practice many aspects of scientific investigation. You will carefully observe, ask questions, make predictions based on your observations and research, use units of metric measure, record information, and analyze what you have seen and done. You will be a scientist!

Read the question. Choose the best answer.

1. Which is <u>not</u> a metric unit of measure?

     o a. meter
     o b. liter
     o c. gram
     o d. inch

2. Which choice lists units of measure from smallest to largest?

     o a. mile, yard, foot, inch
     o b. liter, meter, degree, gram
     o c. millimeter, centimeter, meter, kilometer
     o d. kilogram, gram, milligram

3. To view an insect antenna, which tool would you use?

   o a. ruler
   o b. microscope
   o c. thermometer
   o d. telescope

4. A dime is about as thick as

   o a. 1 millimeter
   o b. 1 meter
   o c. 1 kilometer
   o d. 1 centimeter

5. Which unit of measure would you use to weigh an elephant?

   o a. ounce
   o b. kilogram
   o c. gram
   o d. liter

6. Which metric unit of measure is about the same as a quart?

   o a. pound
   o b. liter
   o c. gram
   o d. degrees Celsius

7. Which of the following is an example of a fact?

   o a. Minerals are not living things.
   o b. It will rain in Los Angeles tomorrow.
   o c. I will roll a four on the dice.
   o d. We will never know whether there is life on Mars.

8. Which of the following is a prediction?

   o a. Minerals are not living things.
   o b. It rains in Washington in the winter.
   o c. I will roll a four on the dice.
   o d. We do not know whether there is life on Mars.

9. Which of the following is an example of a hypothesis?

    o a. A miniature rose bush needs more than 2 hours of light each day to bloom.
    o b. A diamond is a very hard mineral.
    o c. Will a miniature rosebush bloom if it only gets 2 hours of light each day?
    o d. Roses bloom in the summer.

10. Which is <u>not</u> a type of data that scientists usually record?

    o a. observations
    o b. random guesses
    o c. measurements
    o d. patterns that occur

SCIENCE
ANSWER KEY

Physical Science
1. C
2. A
3. B
4. A
5. D
6. A
7. C

Life Science

Plants & Animals
1. C
2. C
3. B
4. C
5. B
6. A
7. A
8. A
9. C
10. D
11. C
12. A
13. D
14. C
15. B
16. B

Life Cycles
1. B
2. D
3. D
4. B
5. C
6. A

Earth Science

Rocks
1. C
2. A
3. D
4. C
5. B
6. A
7. C
8. D
9. A

Rocks, Cont'd.
10. C
11. C

Fossils
1. C
2. B
3. A
4. C
5. A
6. D

Investigations
1. D
2. C
3. B
4. A
5. B
6. B
7. A
8. C
9. A
10. B